TODAY YOU WRITE THE BOOK:
The Keys to Start Your Novel

BEN PARRIS

ALSO FROM BLUEBERRY LANE BOOKS

Books by
Irving A. Greenfield
ANCIENT OF DAYS
WHARF SINISTER
MASS FOR A DEAD WITCH
ONLY THE DEAD SPEAK RUSSIAN
A PLAY OF DARKNESS
SNOW GIANTS DANCING
BEYOND VALOR

Ben Parris
WADE OF AQUITAINE
MARS ARMOR FORGED
CREDS: THE IRS ADVENTURE

Tyne Everett
WALK SMART WALK THIN

Anthologies
DRASTIC MEASURES
WASH THE SPIDER OUT

TODAY YOU WRITE THE BOOK:
The Keys to Start Your Novel

Ben Parris

Blueberry Lane Books
New York
2015

Today You Write the Book: The Keys to Start Your Novel, 2nd Edition
Copyright © 2014 - 2015 by Ben Parris

ISBN 978-1-942183-02-0

Blueberrylanebooks.com

Table of Contents

Introduction: Let's Get Started

It's a great time to be a writer. Source material abounds and is easy to access. A wider array of opportunities to get your work seen exists than ever before. **Yet it's still far more difficult to be a *novelist* than any other kind of writer, and this is why the successful writing of novels maintains its mystique.** The secrets of telling an expansive story in an entertaining way, while you transform yourself into someone who can do that, are the most highly guarded and hardest to convey in all of the entertainment industry. This guide contains some of the nuts and bolts you don't see elsewhere, and gives you the rest of the vital information in a more accessible form.

There are many experienced writers of short pieces who find it nearly impossible to work at novel-length, defeated by the quandary of where to go next with a story fragment. They don't understand plot and complexity.

Then there is the legion of half-educated semi-professionals that have no problem writing a dozen terrible books at novel length. They usually know how to plot but are oblivious that most of their other story elements are missing or poorly executed.

Still others have terrific stories that look like origami in their heads, and cannot be folded into shape with actual paper. Or at least not by them, because writing is ultimately about writing, not just thinking about writing.

There is a whole other category of those who show flashes of greatness at one small aspect of being an author and don't know how to acquire the rest.

This book works for all of these types of writers-in-training.

So we must go back and ask: Why is it so difficult to analyze what novelists do and what *you* must do? If you crave the idea of being a novelist, it is because you love the magic of novels. Most often you sit back with one of your favorite authors and let the enchantment flow over you, mesmerized by the story as a world you can live in. When you stop to examine individual words and sentences, the veneer of pure visualization evaporates. Remembering that the paragraph you examine is a small part of a magnificent structure, you are mystified as to how you would reproduce such complexity, and wonder how you could ever even begin to construct a great work such as the one you hold in your hand.

The truly great novel appears to have been completed as easily as the output of a 3-D printer, layer upon layer of precision treading an unwavering blueprint. It is nothing of the kind. The work is more like molded clay in pursuit of a vision, and even that analogy falls short because novel writing is unique. It is not only unique in the main, but is also a process of infinite variety depending on who is doing the writing, and each stage is arrived upon by experiment.

Writing is invention and art, a way of creating what is uniquely yours. If you are waiting to be told *exactly* how to do such a thing, you will never do it because no one can tell you how to invent *your* story, considering that your own brain is the source.

Like any brainchild, creating is a process of experiment, thought, and further experiment.

Like any art, devising what is uniquely yours is a journey no one else can take. What *can* be learned is the array of elements of traditional and non-traditional techniques that have been successful in pleasing audiences. This book is a practical guide lacking the noise that clogs up an academic course. **But remember, art and invention don't really have rules.** Everything that follows, no matter how it's labeled, is but a SUGGESTION.

Warm regards,
Ben Parris
New York, 2015

The 3 Kinds of Writers
(and How they Succeed)

One of the most common reasons writers get stuck is that they suffer from a lack of insight about themselves. If you wish to delve into writing's deepest mysteries, you must first discover a few crucial things both about yourself and about your readers. If you don't know what kind of writer you are, you will never be able to proceed in an appropriate fashion. An appropriate fashion is a working style that builds upon your strong points. Successful writers may be grouped as follows:

1. **Builders.** These writers, by their nature, "under-write." Those in this category are *minimalists* who taste the cooking constantly to see if that last bit of seasoning did the trick. Also included are those who are writing in a rush of excitement, sharing one idea after the next and avoiding the boredom of explaining at length. Beginning with the outline, Builders gradually fill the novel out with its essential ingredients. Builders who succeed do so because they have turned their nature into a method. The objective of the first step in this method (and all the other important steps that

follow) is to take the outline (see the section on outlining below) and eliminate everything that is so "outlinish" about it, i.e. transform it into story.

How to succeed at being a Builder: Convert your outline into complete and specific sentences, provide the logical connections, and most of all, reveal the story in live action and dialogue instead of summarizing it (this is part of what the famous "show versus tell" means). It's not about a man walking into a bar, it's about Heathcliff Von Stueben staggering into Occam's Bar on 45th and Spindle Avenue because it's his last stop before killing himself. Builders—the under-writers that they are—spend most of their time and energy "revising" by feeding in new details. In order to do this properly, you must have separate character sheets to draw from, and use these to conduct some trial-and-error scenarios that you use to see which versions of your scenes play out properly. Walt Whitman, even though a poet (and pretty much a stranger to traditional publishing, by the way) was the ultimate Builder, adding to and self-publishing new and longer versions of his *Leaves of Grass* throughout his life.

2. **Destroyers.** Any seasoned editor will tell you (in their own terms) that most writers are, of necessity, "Destroyers" or people whose work must be heavily redacted by others in order to "save" them (i.e. make their manuscript *commercially viable*). These writers, by their nature, over-write. They never wanted to be Destroyers, but they are obliged to spend most of their time and energy revising by *subtracting*, taking their natural excess and exuberance and learning to make it concise. They often must be urged to delete whole scenes and whole chapters at a time, as well as portions of the remaining sentences. Where Builders are tentative, Destroyers are expansive. They tend to be wordy and to over-explain their concepts, which is not to say that their work does not sparkle in the end. We are talking about successful writers here who have terrific ideas and know the elements of story, but don't know when they've spilled the wine over the rim of the cup.

How to succeed at being a Destroyer: The successful Destroyer is a master self-editor even before the real editor gets there. If there is too much work left when the manuscript is submitted, the editor will send it back. So the Destroyer must look upon his draft as an enormously valuable block of marble that needs to be mercilessly chipped away to rescue a flawless statue hidden inside. In the final analysis, if not sooner, they must scrutinize their work at the chapter level and then continue to lesser levels of details. Every chapter and scene has to go on trial to discover its purpose. If the author himself does not know a section's purpose, the reader will not know the purpose either.

3. **Geniuses.** Think of Emily Dickinson, who was spurred to greatness by reading greatness. This prescription seems like an easy pill to swallow, but the vast majority of us read greatness and scratch our heads wondering how to reproduce it. We suspect that if we ever do produce our masterpiece it will take a lifetime. Yet the work of a genius writer flows from her pen so quickly that the rough draft may as well have been made of flash paper that burns to nothing behind the trailing scrawl. Maybe there is no draft. Their work is done so fast and so flawlessly that they become prolific and produce a body of work that ranges from serviceable to immortal.

Now think of Charles Dickens. His IQ is estimated to have been 180. He was, then, a genius by any measure, but we're talking about geniuses of the craft, so our list certainly includes people like Tom Clancy, whose writing is streamlined for today's market, and Janet Evanovich, who conquered romance even before she became a giant of contemporary mysteries. What all prodigies have in common is that at one time they were somewhat less perfect and they got better through single minded pursuit of their dreams. Do not confuse Geniuses with perfectionists; a perfectionist's work is never done. A genius meets deadlines (both those that are internally and externally imposed), even while producing professional-grade work.

If you are none of the above, empirical evidence says you should endeavor to become one!

The 3 Kinds of Audiences
(and Which to Pick)

Yes, you can pick, if you wish. You may know your genre well, but do you ever ask yourself who you are writing for? To what end are you shaping your work? That consideration will affect everything about the work you produce, including whether or not you finish your work at all. Hint: Those who write for no one usually do not feel obligated to finish their work. Essentially, you have three choices (other than writing for no one at all):

1. **Writing for "the Masses."** Of the three options, shooting for mass appeal is the worst strategic choice you can make when you are starting out. Who are the masses, anyway? Everyone. And since there is no such thing as a book that everyone wants to read, you will be on an unfocused fool's errand that attracts practically no one. Don't confuse mega-hits for books everyone wants to read. Name any international bestselling book outside of religion, and you'll find billions of people who *still don't* want to read it. Me-too formulations that crank out popular elements (as in, "today I write my Harry Potter") are possible but

imitations are never quite bestsellers. Before best-selling authors were factories they were originals. A fresh approach is what finds the big audiences. If you copy your own formula under those circumstances, you will do well.

2. **Writing for Yourself.** Right or wrong, this is what most books tell you to do. "Can't please everyone so you got to please yourself." This solves the central problem of item number one above (finding a focus) and the approach will work well enough for a while. The trouble is, you yourself may be the optimum audience for your work and then again you may not. If we define true success as the best possible height you can personally reach, it's most likely that you will fall short of true success in that manner because you will keep improving until you amaze yourself into a false sense of security that may actually impede further progress. *Wow, you say to yourself, that's ten times, a hundred times, a thousand times better than I thought I could do.* **In publishing terms, some writer's personal best resembles no objective standard at all.** The work that amuses you so well will probably be somewhat entertaining to others, but not so much that they will have an urge to read it when compared to their other wonderful choices out there. That means yours goes on an enormous "to read" list that your potential audience will

never get down to. If you are philosophical about the idea of drawing pleasure from a personal best, then writing for yourself will be the route to happiness regardless of how many people read your work. If one day this approach no longer works for you because it is not a concrete goal, then you can try the third option.

3. **Writing for a Particular Person (or a well-defined group).** In this instance, you are writing on the basis of: *Person "A" would enjoy my current effort. Or, my work would not meet Person "A's" standard and taste.* And you do not want to disappoint them! The value of this approach is that it makes your work coherent and gives you an objective. Such a focal point is approximately what we used to call a "muse," but the person playing this role can more accurately be described as a sounding board. The approach depends on the subjective evaluation of someone with high standards. This is how Paul Simon wrote when Art Garfunkel was around. This is how Paul McCartney wrote when John Lennon was around. In each case, their lyrics tended to lose intellectual validity when they no longer had their yardstick. They were, of course, still so brilliant that they maintained enormous audiences and crafted vibrant tunes even when

they found themselves at a disadvantage (which is to say when their muse was gone). **Work up to being like them at their best; don't aspire to being a pale copy of their diminished level.** If you want a muse, you need an objective and unwavering standard. Embracing this philosophy does not include the nod of some all-forgiving parent; it embraces the opposite, more like a demanding father or mother you strive to please.

By the way, you and I are not technically allowed to start a sentence with the word "essentially," as I did at the start of this section, saying: "Essentially, you have three choices." An adverb is designed to modify a verb. A good English teacher would ask: What the heck are we modifying in that instance? Nothing. But again, you are a writer, not a grammarian. If it flies, it's your bird. (See my Grammar notes later)

PART I Story Elements

Chapter One

The Key Scene

Even before the outline, a great way to jump into your novel is to begin with the scene that will be your **"key scene,"** i.e. the one that inspires you and sustains your process because the electricity in that scene is so jolting that you just need to build a book around it. This scene is exciting, or weird, or just nagging at you to put it on paper, and it may happen to belong to any part of the book. Let your subconscious flow at this point where passion for idea is the only rule.

The key scene must be pinned down in written form, but it should float in your mind throughout the entire process of planning the book. Once you have the idea drafted, let it serve as a beacon to keep you close to the shoreline without crashing into the rocks. You need never identify the key scene as such if you don't want to, but your audience should be able to identify it themselves as the most central and memorable idea that characterizes the entire book. Most people would say that the key scene in Stephen King's Misery (even with the differences between the book and the movie) was where uber-fan Annie Wilkes decides to "hobble" Paul Sheldon, the author she has kidnapped, so that he remains in her thrall to re-write a novel ending she despised. Look how easy this scene is to describe quickly, and how compelling!

Not every scene ends up working so well. There's an old saying that "there's many a slip twixt the cup and the lip." It may take several tries to select the right scene out of several competing ideas. From there whatever key scene you come up with may not materialize in as "captivating" a form as Stephen King's hobbling scene; most visions become somewhat degraded in the execution. But it must be one that you absolutely love or there is no chance that your readers will.

Description Challenge

In order to test your key scene properly it must not remain in draft form. A strong command of description is essential for fleshing out your scene and bringing it to life. How can the prose inspire you or anyone else if the imagery isn't dazzling?

Some skills are difficult to practice in isolation. Not this one. If you are not already a master of description, you can and should practice this talent on its own, taking the art to absurd lengths for no other reason than to stretch your abilities. Later you can pepper in other writing elements.

But it's not only detail that sells a story. Detail has a first cousin called precision, and the number one enemy of a novice author is imprecision. Sometimes your character can get away with saying, "things just ain't right." But more often—almost always—we readers want to know exactly what those "things" are. Therefore you must practice precision along with detail as if all of the imprecise words you know and love have ceased to exist. We are not speaking of personal pronouns here; those stay when appropriate. We're speaking of eliminating that which is fuzzy.

Read all instructions below in this description practice challenge.

Exercise K1: Find an object in your house and use no less than 500 words to detail everything about it, including its measurements. Furnish your object with a real or fake history. Contrive a way to use all five senses.

Exercise K2: Describe one thing you did yesterday in 750 words of painstaking, excessive detail. What did you mean to do? What actually happened? How did you feel about the outcome?

ALERT: The following words will wink out of existence for the duration of both of these exercises:

It; thing; something; anything; someone; anyone; other;
another;
all; this (if no noun follows); that (if no noun follows).

When the set of exercises is over, you can allow those words to creep back into dialogue when appropriate, and you can allow them back into exposition ONLY when their vagueness is meant to serve a purpose that you could articulate if asked.

Passive Aggressive

Should your descriptions be "active" or "passive"? The common impulse is to say, "Active, of course." But is that always true? Some people absolutely lose their minds tilting at any discussion of the grammatical constructions known as passive voice and active voice. This is the second most heated topic among confused writing students, and even more so if we narrow the field to writing club members of all ages (for the #1 most heated subject, see Exposition Done Right).

It is always the people who have the grammar wrong, however, that shout loudest, and they proceed along the following **two *false* premises**:

a)   That Passive Voice is strictly defined by any use of the word "was"; and

b)   The idea that Passive Voice (even when correctly defined) can *never* be the correct choice.

This topic is poorly taught in most English classes even as it remains of great importance to writers. Therefore this issue will rise to the prominence of our one and only grammar lesson here, albeit limited to what you need to know most.

Grammar Mini-lesson on Passive Versus Active Voice:

Instead of relying on the idea that passive voice is formed whenever the verb "to be" is in play (not entirely true anyway), the concept is better understood as a subject-object reversal.

Subject – The entity taking action or the entity that is directly under discussion.

Object – The entity acted upon, which need not be an inanimate object.

Active: Owen (subject) lit the fire (object).

Passive: The fire (object) was lit by Owen (subject).

> **Analysis:** Owen, as the one lighting the fire, has the role of the traditional sentence subject. He comes first here, providing the classic active order. But in the second version, the focus is on the object—the fire—lending that word the quality of a sentence's subject. Yet Owen is still subject since he is the one taking action. Since he as the subject comes second in this sentence, we call this order passive. All things being equal, the active form is strongly preferred as the passive comes across as more awkward and less dynamic. The author may have a legitimate creative reason, however, for using the passive

form. Suppose that fire was lit every night. Owen swore he would never do it again, but that very day his spirit was broken. Now if you use the active form of the sentence it sounds oddly routine whereas the passive usage shifts the emphasis to the fire where it now belongs, being lit by an appropriately awkward and less dynamic Owen.

Active: Astrid, who was still bitter about the way she'd been treated, liked to find small ways to vandalize the houses where she worked.

Passive: The house was vandalized during its empty winter months.

Analysis: Although the first sentence gives more information, they are both reasonable constructions, depending upon the author's intent. In the passive case, the emphasis is on what happened to the house, and in this case, we don't know who did the vandalizing anyway.

Active: Boston Bob, the mayor himself, astonished everyone when he invited our small army to stay the night.

Passive: Our small, weary army entered the town under a hazy sky and were invited to stay for the night.

Analysis: Again, both are useful, but what else do you notice here? A passive sentence can be dressed up to sound good too. In the second case, the validity of the passive choice comes from the fact that we really don't care who extended the invitation because that person is not going to be important in the story.

Now we get to the real surprises.

Active: I had sixteen business cards from defunct companies in my overstuffed wallet.

Also Active: I *was still* dragging around sixteen business cards from defunct companies in my overstuffed wallet.

Analysis: Here is a case where we use a form of the verb "to be" and there is *no* subject-object reversal, so this is in fact an active sentence, whether loud writing club members like it or not. If you need further proof, you will find hundreds of such sentences in any bestseller.

And lastly, we get to the most surprising case of all.

Not Strictly Passive: "The fire was lit by Owen."

Analysis: Didn't we just say that exact sentence was passive, though? And isn't it judged by the subject-object reversal? No, because we have no call to judge this particular formulation that way. Compare the two similar specimens more carefully. Do you see the tiny difference between them? The difference is that this second version of the sentence is in quotes! It answers the question, "Who was the fire lit by?" No matter how passive the statement would otherwise be, *dialogue* should never be subjected to the same sort of analysis as non-dialogue. This is what the character *said*. You cannot hold a *character* to an objective standard of grammar. The same analysis goes for the utterances of a first-person narrator (which is *all* of the narration!) and even some of the other POV conventions. That particular line may be a terrible idea for any number of reasons, but its appropriateness is dependent on how the character speaks as well as the situation. Maybe you want some of your characters to speak with grammatical correctness. Certainly you would not wish that of all of them. (See Characters Speak)

Chapter Two

The Idea Factory

The idea factory is the author's brain. How well that factory cranks out its product depends—much like a typical manufacturer of goods—on the raw materials, the manufacturing methods and tools, the skilled labor, the product's packaging, and its distribution.

A fresh idea in the right hands, which is to say one approached with a high degree of skill and diligence, is a sack of gold. The chief advantage you begin with is that you have a **unique mind**. You can't help it. Fresh ideas are new combinations of existing ideas with a fresh interpretation.

If you like concepts crystalized into mathematical-style terms, the equation looks like this:

IDEAS + TOOLS + EXPERIENCE + WORK = SUCCESS

In a factory, your methods determine the tools you need, and so it is with writing. We're here to talk about the methods and tools, and to some degree even the material; the experience and the work to follow are entirely up to you.

Where the Factory Falters

Some people have no problem generating ideas, but without the tools, experience and work, they turn their ideas into something useless.

The unsuccessful idea factory usually fails due to the following causes (to be addressed as needed in the rest of the book):

1. Leaving the ideas as raw materials.

2. Waiting so long to get into production that the raw materials are no longer fresh.

3. Making a cheap knock-off product by -
   a. Never refining the raw materials
   b. Failing to use the right tools
   c. Not employing the right skills (mishandling the tools), or
   d. Doing sloppy work.

4. Making a product that no one needs, due to lack of experience. Experience, in this case, is being widely read, because experience will also give you a sense of what readers "need," what they more likely consider original.

Where the Factory Flourishes

With the above pitfalls in mind, we resolve to avoid them by absorbing the lessons of this book, and turn to your next exploitable advantage: **Literacy**. The experience part of the equation actually has two components: both reading and writing. You must practice writing, but your success will also depend upon the extent to which you are literate. Some people are natural mimics, finding it easy to reproduce a version of what they've just read. But employing mimicry is a sword that cuts both ways: You want to be able to reproduce working formulas, but strict copying yields the opposite of creativity.

If we accept the ancient proposition that all ideas exist already, then what you are doing is choosing the right idea for the right treatment at the right time. You are making these choices because your extensive reading has helped guide you past choosing the ideas that have oversaturated the current market. And don't forget your unique mind, because this is what you use to refine the raw materials. Yours may be refined in a superior manner to those of your competitors.

But let's say that you are *not* one of those people who can swim through a sea of ideas that are "all out there somewhere."

How do you become one?

First you need to suspect that you can get the ideas to coalesce for you, and ask yourself where this suspicion comes from. Perhaps, for example, you've put some great stories and scenes together before and now you find yourself blocked.

What we know of the left brain and right brain are usually treated as momentarily amusing concepts that writers can afford to bandy about on social media and then dismiss. Right brain: Creative-intuitive. Left brain: Math and organizational skills. When examined at the biological level, success is about how well you access both sides of the brain, depending on what you are trying to do.

With creative works, you need ample access to the right side of your brain and a way of getting there when the path is turned off. Here are ten tried and true methods of opening that path:

1. **Read a novel.** This is especially important if you've just come home from work. Even though a novel represents someone else's creativity and is already set in place, it demonstrates the creative process, carries you away from your current circumstances, and causes you to wonder what will happen next in the story, which itself is a creative process.

2. **Lie down for a moment.** Being horizontal usually takes you a step closer to a dream state. In the transitional period where your body prepares for sleep, you stop thinking of immediate actions you need to take. If you are

prone to insomnia, however, you probably do not stop thinking in terms of immediate actions, but you still have many other options to shake off writer's block.

3. **Go for a walk.** Being in motion switches on your imagination because you must be prepared to anticipate dangers in your environment.

4. **Go for a drive.** Here you are in quicker motion and must think faster. If you are a new driver, this method will probably not work, as you may need to put a great deal of conscious thought into what you are doing.

5. **Take a bath.** In this instance you are horizontal or approximately so, and you are surrounded by water, which can carry some degree of danger and therefore opens the imagination.

6. **Take a shower.** In a shower you are vertical, but the water is flowing in a manner reminiscent of a waterfall. If you were standing naked in a waterfall you would certainly have to be attuned to danger, which is an imagination state.

7. **Assemble a collage.** Challenging the mind to find arrangements of physical shapes is no different from arranging ideas.

8. **Meditate.** Meditation, over the long run, is a practiced manner of changing your state of mind which involve (at a minimum) shedding the immediate concerns that block you.

9. **Bounce a ball** (Paul Simon's creativity method). Bouncing a ball is not the strictly repetitive action that it seems. Ensuring that your hand meets the ball every time requires a calculation that takes place below the surface of your thoughts.

10. **Lucid dream** (takes years of practice). Lucid dreaming is being able to extend some degree of conscious control to a mental state that is typically the province of your unconscious mind. You make the sort of decisions that your conscious mind would make as the otherwise unpredictable dream world flows around you. Non-lucid dreaming may occasionally produce material for your writing (provided you remember your dreams), but lucid dreaming is a more desirable state where you bring some organization to the free flow of ideas, which is very much what creative writing is all about. Even where the lucid dream does

not directly produce what you need, you awaken in a state that is more conducive to writing. Whatever kind of dreaming you do, most professional writers surveyed find that they do their best work in the morning when concerns of the day have not yet clouded their thinking. Others cannot work until they have gotten the day's tasks over with.

All of the efforts above will, to some degree, engage your corpus callosum, which connects the two sides of your brain—the left with its language and logic, and the right with its intuition and creativity. You have to think like a marching army—RIGHT-LEFT-RIGHT—when you acquire ideas, get them on paper and then improve them.

Practice reinforcing your natural tendency to look at things your own way instead of copying others and there will come a time when you no longer struggle for originality. This effort requires global discipline, meaning that it must be something that you do all the time and in all situations. Even in the most casual communication you must not succumb to cliché or you will never climb out of the habit. If you maintain a tight discipline, barring clichés for long enough, you will one day be awash in ideas, and your main problem will be how to manage them all.

If none of the above work—EVER—then you may not be a writer after all. Let's take a brief, unscientific, personality test for fun to see what track you may actually be on. Write down a yes or no answer to each question and use the scorecard below.

1. Being an author is what I've always wanted.

2. I have completed at least one short story.

3. I can write at length without any help.

4. I lock my manuscripts in a safe because I know they are *that* valuable.

5. I can write at length only if I think of someone as my muse.

6. I can write at length only if I have a writing partner.

7. I can progress in my writing only by lifelong revision of earlier works.

If your answers were: 1-yes; 2-yes; 3-no; 4-no; 5-no; 6-yes; 7-no, then congratulations, you are: Harper Lee

If your answers were: 1-yes; 2-yes; 3-yes; 4-no; 5-no; 6-no; 7-yes, then congratulations, you are: Walt Whitman

If your answers were: 1-yes; 2-yes; 3-yes; 4-yes; 5-no; 6-no; 7-no, then congratulations, you are: Stephen King

If your answers were: any other combination, then congratulations, you are: Unknown quantity. An unknown quantity has unlimited potential, so that's not bad at all.

Back to business... No matter what kind of an author you are, once you have ideas in play, and long before you have developed them all, you will want to begin working on your outline. Your outline will be partly done if you first write down your plot.

Chapter Three

What Is Plot?

We often say, "I have an idea for a story," but there is no such thing. Remember:

An Idea is *Not* a Story

An idea may graduate to that lofty level if you find it a useful starting point around which you add in a plot. What some of us mean to say by the careless notion of "idea for a story" is: "I've thought of an interesting situation that I think I can develop into a story, novel, or play." "Develop" is the key word here.

The novice who believes that an idea really *is* a story spends their life wondering why nothing ever came of their precious notion.

An idea is: A man falls in love with a computer program. Good idea (and lots of people had it). If you don't know what "happens," then you don't have a plot, which means you are not really on your way to a story, and you shouldn't reasonably feel distressed if someone else goes and writes a story that you didn't write.

A plot is: the course of the story, a picture of a traveled path told in words. And a destination! Plots are dots, each dot a scene which is part of a bigger picture. Thus the saying, "every picture tells a story." When the path is linear, fewer dots may suffice. When the path curves, you need more points of reference in order to define the contours of that curve. Once you have the points of reference, label those dots and ask yourself how you want to get your characters from one point to the next, and most importantly, to the conclusion. Do you then have a viable plot? Not necessarily.

Plots are built around introduction, conflict, and resolution. "Comedy" used to mean a story with a happy ending, where the protagonist was better off than he started out, and "tragedy" meant a story with a sad ending, wherein the protagonist was worse off than he started, usually much worse. Notice that we don't say that the ending is the opposite of the beginning. Think of the tragedy Hamlet. The beginning of that story was not good at all. His father had just died, possibly at the wicked hand of his uncle Claudius. While Hamlet has a simple solution in mind to expose Claudius, real life proves to be so complex that virtually nothing goes right and virtually no one survives.

Whatever you label them today, those two paths of comedy and tragedy—better off or worse off at the end—are still the most popular scenarios.

Saved by the Arc

In modern novels, plots are said to have a **story arc**, which is a term that helps us visualize the construction and deconstruction of a "rising and falling" central conflict, not to mention smaller conflicts along the way.

Rising action is sometimes defined as a chain of incidents building toward the point of greatest "interest." While this is a somewhat useful definition, it implies that the remainder of your book (the falling action) is going to be increasingly *un*interesting. Needless to say, the conclusion of your novel ought *not* to be uninteresting!

Another, clearer, way to begin this definition is that the rising action is characterized by events that are building up tension. But then you must ask, in what way? The functional construction is to say that rising action includes events that make it increasingly unlikely that the hero will ever reach his or her goal. Ahhhh! The word "rising" in this formulation corresponds to higher and higher hurdles to jump over, making you wonder at which point it is beyond our hero's prowess and endurance to prevail.

Putting it all together, rising action is about increasing obstacles that place the goal further out of reach, thus causing the tension (assuming that we want the hero to succeed).

If we reduce the picture to a diagrammatic arc, you would think that the proportions of that arc would be significant. Yet academic explanations based on the "story pyramid" mistakenly show story structure as proportionate when in fact the rising action is by far the longest part of the book.

Some definitions beg the question by saying that the rising action is the part of the story that is on the way to the climax. Awful definition, the worst yet. Good thing we already have a better one.

But this leads to the question: What is the **climax**? Dictionary.com has the climax in literature as "a decisive moment that is of maximum intensity or is the major turning point in the plot." Not bad, though dictionaries are always sparing. We still have a way to go to figure it out.

Other sources tell us that climax is the "peak of the crisis," the turning point between rising action and falling action. That location-based description tells us where we are on the arc diagram and little else. Which part of that information, if any, is useful for writing? Well if we take the "peak of the crisis" to mean the most difficult part for our hero to surmount, then it becomes clearer that the climax is what the rising action was setting up.

But employing words like "moment" and "peak" in regard to the climax are highly misleading, especially when you leave out the fact that the resolution is part of the climax. What's more, the climax in modern literature is understood to satisfy your expectations, so that must be part of the definition. If that were not so, there would be no such term as anti-climax.

Anti-climax is the sense of having been cheated out of your expectations by either a trivial solution to the big problem, or not overcoming the problem at all (the hero dies and by implication fails to be the hero). Since this can be a major plot flaw, this juncture in plot is worth examining in detail.

H.G. Wells' *The War of the Worlds* is sometimes cited as having an anti-climactic ending because a common Earth virus defeats the aliens instead of an action by the protagonist defeating them. Yet this is considered a classic, and often revisited story. If we are speaking of satisfaction, the audience experiences an enormous sense of relief that humanity was not destroyed; that in itself is a form of satisfaction (See also The Ending You So Richly Deserve and the Sum of All Strengths). If readers and viewers are happy, this is probably not the best example of anti-climax.

In Will Smith's version of *I Am Legend* (2007), he kills himself at the end of the climax, and apparently does so for no good reason.

We all know how grenades work, Will! You can throw it and then get into the coal chute with the others. You don't have to blow up with it!

I Am Legend (2007) set records at the box office so one could argue that it wasn't a clear example of anti-climax either. This financial success, however, is less of a mystery when you note that:

1. the anti-climax was mitigated when Smith saved two other people and the world, so he dies *and* accomplishes his goal;

2. the plot followed the precept that the hero must pay a great price for victory;

3. that there was an alternate ending where the hero does *not* die; and

4. that Will Smith is big box office regardless of plot flaws.

No writer creates an anti-climax (disappointment) on purpose right? They don't. The screenwriters for 2007's *I Am Legend* were probably trying to replicate the ending of *Beneath the Planet of the Apes* where Taylor destroys the world and himself with the ultimate atomic bomb. But in his case it was clear that this outcome was his only choice. He didn't know that there was a time machine handy.

Audiences were disappointed in losing Charlton Heston, but the irony worked because his character, Taylor, had been angry that the bomb had been used before! Plus, the audience could not be sure there would be further sequels anyway. The very next sequel, *Escape from the Planet of the Apes*, did all right (though not as well as with Heston) because it turned out that two of our favorite character-protagonists were the ones who found the time machine, and this logic (even if a paradox), tied in to the overall story arc since they also turned out to be the ones who started Earth down the path of the ape future.

I Am Legend parallels the original *Planet of the Apes* franchise yet it does so without the logic. Trying to adapt another story's logic to your story is one way that anti-climax can accidentally end up in a final script.

If we think of the anti-climax as short-circuiting the tension, another component that causes a drop in tension is something that might be termed the **Mini-anti-climax**. While this is often confused for anti-climax, it is nothing of the kind since it occurs quite naturally during the rising action.

The quintessential Mini is what I call the cat-under-the-baseball-bat. The scenario goes like this: Our hero, or more likely a lesser character who will soon be killed, has reason to be frightened, so when she hears a sound behind the door, she raises a bat to strike her attacker, presumably a male who is taller than her. As she aims high, and opens the door with her foot, the harmless cat scoots past her feet. It meows and she sighs.

The purpose of occasionally reversing your rising tension is to mimic real life, where nothing goes in a perfectly straight line, and to put your protagonists off guard with softballs even when the signs say they should know better. The viewer knows perfectly well that the danger is not over.

Falling action, which follows the climax, can best be described as the portion of your story that takes place after the *main* problem has been solved (it is not enough to say that we have resolved the conflict because we have not resolved *all* conflict). To adopt this definition, the main problem must have been disposed of *during* the climax, and all the lesser issues are dealt with afterward. Falling action forms a bridge to the ultimate resolution and ties up loose ends along the way.

Note also that in the falling action, one of the main tasks is to sort out the *effects* of the climax. At this stage, cliché is not only tolerated; it may, in some contexts, be mandatory. For example, if you are writing the first of the Star Wars movies, your protagonists *must* be awarded medals at the end in order to meet the emotional expectation that goes with the flavor of the film.

So we've got rising action, climax, and falling action. Are we missing any literary elements? According to some sources, yes. Gustav Freytag's nineteenth century analysis of five-act plays by the ancient Greeks and Shakespeare is still floating around. He would say that we are missing exposition (claimed to precede rising action), and denouement, which supposedly follows the falling action. These two elements sit at the feet of a pyramid (yes, he articulated the nineteenth century obsession with pyramids), a shape that does not represent modern fiction in which rising action is a long line and falling action a short one. Five-act dramatic structure is worth mentioning here only because some people mistakenly believe that it can still be shoehorned into three-act play structure, applied in the case of a novel to the beginning, middle and end.

To adapt Freytag's analysis, the first part of the beginning would be where all the exposition is located. This is certainly not true today. (See Exposition Done Right, and Timing in particular). He also had the major resolution located in the falling action rather than in the climax (no wonder everyone is confused about where that element goes!), and **denouement** designated as a separate final scene after the falling action. This last is a concept worth mentioning because it represents the measuring point for where all the characters end up. It would contain the final resolution, final catastrophe, if any, and any revelation that comes to light. This is actually part of falling action but can still be the last scene.

By the time you are through plotting, or ending up with a fully realized plot on the fly (though it is not advisable that you proceed without a complete outline), the story arc is well hidden and the picture is more like the connect-the-dots analogy above. Most importantly, once all of the writing is filled in around those dots, the reader should see a painting and need not be distracted by the underlying structure.

Whether or not the reader sees it, the author still has to know her story arc, and don't you forget it. See the sections below on Beginning, Middle and Ending to learn how a plot should develop. But first, acquaint yourself with your characters and start your outline based on the plot ideas you have so far. Why? The short answer is that the plot ought to be shaped by the characters as well as other factors.

Building Sophistication

Once you have assembled your major plot elements, the production of which is essentially an intellectual exercise in structure, you have gone a long way toward having organized your story. Yet that plot must at some point turn into the fire breathing dragon, or the heart pounding thriller, or the torrid tale of romance it was meant to be. Think of your task as construction work requiring both structure and beauty. For these two elements, you will need the following, respectively:

Load-bearing beams – Your plans for beginning, middle and ending (more to come on those subjects), along with your set of scene descriptions with their aims outlined.

Wallboards and finish - As soon as you can, panel over the above with artful devices, which, from a plot standpoint, would be your explanations of how your character's motivations mesh with their actions in the outlined scenes. (See Characters are People).

Strengthening Plot

As an author you are not just doing the grunt work. You are in fact the architect of a new, and experimental design each time. What if the plot point you depended on turned out not to be a load-bearing beam at all? What if the pixel in your tapestry of a glorious stallion looks more like a loose thread to you? If you can think of nothing better to replace it with, then the answer is to strengthen it by weaving that thread back in. Do more with it. Treat that moment as a building block which you then take further later in the plot.

If you stay alert to the possibility of resurrecting earlier points, you can make the seemingly unimportant into something terribly important.

That troublesome thread may then turn out to be your best point instead of your worst. For examples of spinning plot threads into gold, read any book by Kurt Vonnegut Jr. He was the greatest fan and the greatest master of the recurring plot point, and is said to have figured out the plot for his *Sirens of Titan* on a dare at a party in a single night. The recursive nature of that plot arises from an exploring man and his dog caught in a quantum mechanical "wave phenomena" that causes them to exist in a time and space spiral wherein they reappear on Earth at 59-day intervals.

If you manage to build up a plot point, then work even harder to ensure that the scene that initially includes it is well written with entertaining characterization, dialogue, description, and proper exposition. Vonnegut made his improbable premise real by opening his book with a dramatic illustration of the moment of one of the appearances of the man and dog, imbuing the event with every bit of the nail-biting mystery it deserved. Readers will forgive a great deal of implausibility if they are entertained, because entertainment is their goal.

A second, less important story running alongside a novel's main story is known as a **sub-plot**. It most often involves the less important characters but it could also be a less important series of events happening to your main characters, the real-life issues that burn energy while trying to reach the main goal.

The subplot can either strengthen the main plot by turning out to be consequential in resolving the main conflict or it can remain separate and bolster the plot by echoing the theme—the king and the peasant each struggling with similar problems that fit their level and are dealt with in their own appropriate way. The subplot can be quite serious and its use is an essential ingredient in showing real life. For example, if your main plot is not a love story, you may still want the subplot to be a love story. If your main plot *is* a love story, the subplot can be someone else's love story.

Note that subplots need their own arc with rising and falling action and a climax in between; the story's setting, no matter how elaborate, and all the incidental matters, are not substitutes for an actual subplot. Although inclusion of a subplot while you are focused on the "real" story may start out the hardest planning you do, its development will eventually become automatic.

Chapter Four

Characters are People

Characters are people. The theory and practice of this one concept is most of what you need to know. If you don't understand people, you ought not to be a writer. Readers pick up a story for their own reasons, and in the modern world, the largest portion only pick up a book if they enjoy the characters. They must love to love them or love to hate them.

All essential human traits apply to characters. Those who populate novels are self-interested, possess both good and bad points, and usually have multiple side-interests. They can be loosely based on someone you know or a blend of people you know, or know about, but they must follow some kind of internal (even if complex) logic formed of the patterns of human nature.

That doesn't mean that the answer to character construction is to use a copy of someone you know. Authors who try to base characters too closely on someone they know for the sake of convenience face trouble. Aside from lawsuits, the writing reason for avoiding clones of real life people is that they don't fit neatly into your story and allow you the freedom to write it; they straightjacket your story and steer it in undesirable directions. Characters are allowed to surprise you but they must do so in a way that works. You also want to have the right character for the right story. The chances that this person you know, randomly belongs in the story you are writing now are scant. Do you really suppose that Shakespeare knew a girl like Juliet who was so remarkably impulsive that she actually killed herself in response to the mere appearance of her boyfriend's death? Probably not.

Inventory of Needs

The more central your character to the story, the more that you and the reader must know about them. Character sheets are your custom-made "bibles" regarding each major or repeated character, preferably including:

- o Physical Description
- o Personal history
- o Psychological make-up
- o Motivations and goals

Physical Description

There are three major approaches to physical description, each of them favored by one type of reader or another. The one you choose, and how frequently and thoroughly the description is repeated, is often driven by a study of the genre (which helps you know which type of reader you are serving), but there is enormous variation due to author preference. Here is a sampling of the range of solutions:

1. Voluminous detail provided at one time, or split among a couple of passages. (Some readers feel that they absolutely cannot proceed with a story without a full picture of the characters, including all of their clothing.) The more important a character is, the more detailed their description must be.

2. A prominent feature for the reader to take hold of, such as the "lantern jaw" of Tom Clancy's main protagonist, or the protruding teeth of Bunny in Irwin Shaw's *Rich Man Poor Man*.

3. No description, but for that which the reader might think is implied by their name or profession, plus little hints dropped throughout the book about their general size or hair color. (Some readers say that they prefer to imagine a set of characteristics on their own.)

Personal History

In the terminology we will use here, there are two types of history found in a quality story:

1. *Expository History*, consisting of past events, facts and skill sets explicitly explained or alluded to because they are relevant to the current plot and will become more so later; and

2. *Implied History*, consisting of the sort of data that more broadly shapes personality, behavior and motivation. Most implied history is absorbed by the reader through observation of the character's dialogue and actions. If you put all of this detail into exposition in what is known as an "info dump," readers will be bored and annoyed, and they will forget the information anyway because there is too much and it is not yet relevant. For example, let's say that your character is home-schooled. This might be the one thing you say about her up front, provided that this is a fact that the reader must know immediately. It may be more relevant that she has become a professional wrestler, in which case the author's knowledge that the character is home-schooled will be sufficiently communicated through subtle emotional or behavioral elements imparted to the character, all of which will "make sense" to the reader later, if and when they ever get this fact.

Psychological Make-up

In real life, good people have some bad traits and evil people have some good traits. That's already an oversimplification, but it's better than forgetting that no one is without their "other side," or simply a set of strengths and weaknesses.

Readers want to see personal growth in a story and you can use the weaknesses of the protagonist as something to overcome by the end.

The **villain(s)**, of course, can also overcome weaknesses or gain strength. They can have likeable qualities as well as unlikeable qualities. Most authors find it harder to develop the villain into a fully realized person. If you struggle with this problem, note that the villain is the antagonist, the opposition. A villain with no strengths is no opposition at all and is therefore <u>not</u> a villain. The easiest way to develop a natural set of traits is to ignore for a while which role they play.

It is useful to think of an antagonist as someone whose interests conflict with those of your protagonist. If in real life you think that everyone who disagrees with you is stupid it means that you are unaccustomed to doing a proper, dispassionate analysis of the various other reasons for conflicting viewpoints, but perhaps you can be more objective in your fiction. Even if you are not going to use scenes from the villain's point of view, you should still write them. The best authors are the best students of human nature. Find out to your own satisfaction why your villains—as well as your heroes—behave as they do. Also know how they got to the position they have attained even if you never spell that out.

Try This: To create believable characters you have to get to the core of what *you* can write best. The path to what you do best goes through what you *like* best. Stop for a moment and list what is it you like about your favorite characters in television shows, movies and books. Don't copy; learn principles with which you can design your own character. Once you have a set of traits to work with, take a few pages to let your mind wander over the character to lay out an unstructured biography and philosophy told in their own voice. How she speaks is a window into her soul.

Then you will begin to see if the various traits you have chosen can hang together in a coherent and logical way. If not, they will need adjustment. (If the result still turns out to be a copy of an existing character, redouble your efforts to learn principles of character development—commonalities, not specifics.)

Motivation/ Goals

Motivations, big and small, should be expository, immediate, and repeated. Everyone has something they want, something they need, something they work toward that constantly drives them. If your characters do not have these things, then they are not real people. Long-term and short-term motivations are not necessarily the same thing as big and small wishes. A small but long-term wish may be to go to that next baseball game for which you have purchased lifetime seats.

How long will your reader tolerate your characters not being real people? Not for a minute. The sooner you start spilling motivations of any size, the better.

Try this:

1. List five big motivations any character might have.

2. Continue the list with ten small motivations a character might have

Do one list for protagonists and another for antagonists. Do you notice that they have a lot in common? Now list motivations that your specific characters would naturally have.

Once you know your characters, it is safe to settle on the story's *point of view.* Meanwhile, do the following character exercises relating to what you have learned in this entire chapter.

Actions

A character is nothing without characterization. You must be able to *demonstrate* who they are. People show who they are mainly through their actions (and reactions) because actions are less guarded than speech. People reveal something about themselves, their motivations or their immediate intentions at virtually every moment of every day.

Examples:
- The old woman exiting the church sneered at the young couple as they kissed in public;
- When the bricklayer finished the last swipe of his trowel, he found a tiny hole in the cement which he backfilled with a bit he found on the metal's edge;
- When Edward walked out of the convenience store, he noticed a fleck of blood on his white shirt, which he quickly covered up before the cop across the street got any closer.

In each case above, it should be obvious to you what each case reveals about the selected character in a single sentence, and the message must reach your reader on at least a subconscious level.

Exercise C1: Think of someone that you know, whose behavior you have had difficulty understanding, and make up an explanation for that particular behavior or a broader observation about how they interact with the world. The explanation should be plausible and should be drawn from what you know about them, a narrow band of speculation rather than a wide one. Give them a different name, first and last, before you begin.

Exercise C2: Take someone you have heard about in the news who was convicted of a crime. Refresh your memory of the facts and then write a scene that reveals their motive to the reader but not to any other story character. The easiest way to do that is to use their point of view or an omniscient point of view and consider the examples above as a hint, but you still have a long way to go. Use either the facts as you know them or anything you can imagine. Make sure you include motivations and conflict. See if you can do both a long version and a short version of this exercise. Which way do you find more challenging?

Chapter Five

The Art of Seeing
(Point of View)

Point of view (POV) in art is a reflection of where the artist is standing when painting the picture. In narrative, POV can take any combination of these major forms:

1. If the artist is standing directly in the skin of the protagonist, then the **first-person** "I" is employed. Here you get the 100% strength of unfiltered thoughts and descriptions in a constant stream, so that person we are all inhabiting had better be both interesting and comfortable for the reader to live inside. With first-person POV you are most likely to run into the so-called "unreliable narrator," where the reader must interpret the extent to which the character is providing an accurate story. Unreliable narration is a perfectly reasonable state of affairs because any character in any story can fail to tell the truth because they either don't know the reality of a situation or don't wish to accept the implications. One caveat in this area is that some readers don't recognize

that they are listening to an unreliable narrator, just as people in real life can find themselves relying on someone they shouldn't.

2. No sensible author uses the **second-person**, "you," except for very short stretches, as in the set up to choose-your-own-adventure-type stories. (Or for any set of instructions; in other words, <u>not</u> a story) When used in a complete story, it has a strong tendency to be irritating.

3. The **third-person**, "he" or "she," is the most versatile, allowing for the following possible scenarios and caveats:

   a. Standing close enough to the person to be a conjoined twin (where you will get as close as possible to the same perspective as your hero as you can without actually being that person). This is the most frequently chosen mode. It allows you to describe everything in the way the character sees it, their close perspective, almost in the way they might have described it out loud, rather than their thoughts. The "voice" remains that of the author because the method subtly enhances the language and manner in which the POV character relates the story in order to bring it up to a comfortable standard.

b. Even closer, where you have a conjoined brain and the freakish ability to occasionally read and share with us that person's thoughts (a remarkably common method). Here you occasionally expose their first person thoughts word-for-word in real time using a blended POV.

c. Flitting about so that you hang at the shoulder of various people that change with the chapters, producing the same effect as in (a) and (b). How often you switch is a storytelling choice; or

d. Standing far away from everyone with the power of an omniscient (a rare talent these days). The author has the option to share every character's perspective simultaneously (usually one paragraph to the next) without waiting for a section, scene or chapter switch, and can even provide the motivations of an entire group or speak of the collective events of a time period. The omniscient also expresses things that the character at hand cannot know, such as how the future will treat them or someone else they are dealing with. This is also called **Third-person omniscient**, and if not managed properly can turn into an incoherent muddle. The great masters of this mode, such as Arthur C. Clarke, start with omniscient at the opening of the book and then come down to earth and settle into an individual character. They often return to omniscient at the end.

4. Changing point of view within a scene (especially when not part of a coherent omniscient approach) is usually a disaster. Even when very talented professional authors try this they need an equally talented editor to fix it!

5. An author usually signals which character's point of view will be portrayed by beginning the scene with an action or a thought of that character. If the author begins by telling something about character B, it is very difficult to convince an audience that the scene is really about character A, unless the objective is to consistently jump around like that, but see #4 above.

6. Do not use a pronoun at the outset, thinking that you will tease for a few sentences before telling which character you are talking about. Readers hate this kind of tease because it prevents them from picturing what is going on; when you don't know which character is in play you don't know their motivation. A somewhat

more acceptable variation of this tease is to provide atmospheric information before showing which character is there. There are professional authors that do this without realizing that some readers are forced to read it all over again once they know the identity of the person joining the scene.

Therefore, POV is all about limiting and filtering perception. Don't tell us that Jocelynn was in the habit of being careless of other people's feelings. She doesn't see herself that way!

Chapter Six

Outlining and Order

Do you hate to produce an outline? Get physically unwell at the thought of rendering your entire novel into a single block of cold exposition? Regress to the consistency of a jellyfish while bogged down in the middle of it? Then congratulations. You may be a novelist. A novelist wants to tell stories as only a novelist can, not produce the bloodless scraps a dog wouldn't eat.

Nevertheless, an accursed outline of some kind and dimension is critical for practically all writers, and essential if you want to send your proposal to any agent who insists on an outline before investing in a read of the entire manuscript. This is true of agents that value their time, which as far I know, is all of the good ones.

The agent may instead call for a *synopsis*, which carries the connotation of being shorter and less formal. But any requester following up on your query will usually tell you what length your submission must be. They will tell you outline length and number of chapters. If you they don't specify outline length in their communication to you (and don't say so on their website or in any of their catalog listings), the safest course is to provide both a one-page synopsis and a multi-page detailed outline (and you really should have both on hand anyway). If they don't dictate how many chapters must be part of the submission, it's because they want you to decide at which point in your first three or four chapters you have drawn the reader in. If you cannot figure that out, the agent may reasonably doubt your instincts as a novelist.

Loose and Tight Outlines

Remember that we said your outline will be partly done if you first write down your plot. We weren't kidding. Write out your plot to your personal satisfaction, and remember that you still have more work to do. Some writers prefer loose outlines that, at a minimum, *tell the purpose of each chapter, who is in it, and what their motivation is.*

Other writers will do scene-by-scene work. Tight outlines have everything, preparing for *all of the logic that connects the actions in each scene in the book.* The one that suits you best will get you through the task. Each will provide ample foundation for meeting an agent's requirements *and* for marketing material.

Of course we speak of agents here as part of your motivation even though you may not be seeking one. But the fact is, those who only do a loose outline or none at all, must be a master of on-the-fly management. This constant attention to management means that, at the least, you must as ask yourself why each scene exists as you conjure it into your head in terms of what plot purpose it serves. If a scene serves no useful purpose, you must realize that it is a bad idea to keep it.

First and Last Chapters

Personally, I begin with a *key scene* for inspiration, write a loose, plot-inspired outline (that I update as I go along), and then write a simple draft of the first and last chapters of the book before proceeding with the rest. If anything in between demands my attention, I write it down in whatever detail occurs to me before I forget. Then I string together everything belonging to the intervening territory, crafting the plot as I go and re-envisioning whatever did not work.

Other professionals I've interviewed feel they must proceed in strict sequence while still others have such detailed outlines that they can jump to a section of a scene at any point at any time. Enviable!

Outlining as a Manifestation of Plot

You are not outlining entirely for the sake of an agent; you are outlining to get the book done. **At the very least you ought to know where you are going, and by what means, if you are ever going to get there.** Outlining can be thought of as detailing the plot, the intermediate step between plotting and writing the story. Those who can do without this sort of road map are the rarest of writers. Find the right outline style for you and the river of accomplishment can flow.

Here's a secret that you may find startling, though: Outlines should not be entirely stuffy. While outlines appear to be an inversion of "show, don't tell"—the very opposite of everything we've learned about storytelling—they need not be 180 degrees different from our normal working style. You can allow some details to sneak in here and there. Outlining is not an attempt at journalism. It is more like a vision of what is to come. As far as possible within the restrictions of summary, the outline should be an exciting description of events. You make it so by not succumbing to the tendency to use deadening neutral adjectives, vague or missing nouns, and flat verbs. That means you shouldn't try to maintain academic neutrality. Characters in your outline need not "remark" about significant moments; let them "boast" if they must. Your explanations in an outline may not be blow-by-blow, but don't put away all of the tools of the creative writer.

Lastly, however, you must not be a slave to your outline. Sometimes where we outline, or manifest the plot, we make boneheaded mistakes that simply don't turn out to make sense in the context of the story and the likely decisions of the protagonist. You see it when you "live through" the book and have written up to the point in question. The best craftsmen are terrific at troweling over these cracks in the cement. Even if you were a top-notch artist (which you are not yet), your book is far better off if it makes logical sense in a way that has not been forced.

Flexible plotting is easier if you try a loose outline first, but even if you have progressed past a loose outline to a detailed one, you have to keep your mind flexible. If your rapidly developing instinct says that a plot point is not correct, then do not work towards it; change it and change whatever is necessary after that. Redoing the outline is a small price to pay for having a novel that makes sense.

Chapter Seven

Characters Speak
(Dialogue)

There is a less urgent need for your characters to speak before the stage at which you have the plot, the character backgrounds, and the outline under development. Therefore we held off the discussion of dialogue to this point, but you have not fully discovered your characters until you know what they sound like and why.

Dialogue that readers admire is a function of real-life ramblings punched up and streamlined for relevance and brevity, but not so far streamlined that it unfolds information too quickly for the reader to absorb. If we refer to each portion found in quotes— anything from a paragraphs-long diatribe to a single word—as a "speech," you will want to break up your speeches into shorter snippets whenever they are meant to serve an expository or emotional function. This can be done, as appropriate, by breaking up speeches with actions and/or having the speakers "take more turns." So, for example, instead of your character asking for a favor, and then plunging ahead and describing that favor in the same breath, he can pause for the other character to react to the idea in their own characteristic way.

How do you know when the words are "real"? Real life dialogue is colored by who we are. Everyone is from somewhere, has an occupation or set of activities, finds themselves at a certain stage in life, is possessed of certain needs, and has a particular attitude, and all of these things are reflected in our speech. Therefore, the better you understand regional and socioeconomic differences, the more your characters will ring true.

The Role of Dialogue

In addition to being realistic and illuminating, dialogue should do any of the following:

1. Help develop the character (which includes voice)
2. Move the plot along
3. Both at once (try to choose both)

Common problem of the novice:

A young writer hears that dialogue must draw strict distinctions between characters who converse with each other, and then produces the following desperate attempt at good writing:

"It's nice to see you, mon," said Marinda, a Jamaican woman.

"Yeah mate, it's been six chunders for me since we got together," answered the Australian man, tucking his knife deeper into his belt so as not to seem too threatening.

"Much obliged, pardner," said the Texan, Bob "Ten-Gallon" Pendergast, sneaking up from on them from behind but betraying himself with the stench of oil.

"All of you up and a-boot?" laughed the friendly Canadian coming to join the growing group on deck.

While not a completely incompetent effort, the above stereotyping will entertain a handful of over-insulated people and flounder with regular readers. The writer who serves up such purple dialogue will say that they "learned" that this approach is *the* way to do it. What they've actually done is mis-learned through their misinterpretation of good advice about giving the characters a clear voice.

If it's not already obvious, here's why this kind of writing is a problem: The writer who relies on gimmicks never learns subtlety. Therefore the lazy writer cannot handle a situation where two similar characters must talk to each other. Unless you are producing a series of parody books, only a rare circumstance would provide an international mix to fall back on, and the exchange above grows tiresome over the course of a novel. **Even in a story that takes place at the United**

Nations, you want meaningful contrast, not superficial contrast. Also, if you insist that they all be "colorful" characters, you run the risk that none of them will be seen as colorful characters.

Two or more of your players can come from the same exact background and have entirely different personalities and interests such as avid meat eaters versus staunch vegetarians. Or lawyers who love what they do, and others who despise themselves for it. Find natural contrasts and conflicts. They exist!

Dialogue Drivers

Bearing in mind that the reader wants to "see" which character is speaking at any given time and never wants to feel confused about who is saying what, the following list provides some of the tools authors use to differentiate character dialogue (other than verbal gimmicks) so that the reader can recognize the speakers:

1. **Motivation**. Characters will necessarily talk about their needs and desires, once established, and thus be identified by such dialogue content.

2. **Broad perspective**. Those who are older, younger, more experienced, and less experienced in the task at hand are major determinants of how people speak.

3. **Narrow perspective**. Verbalizing immediate needs will further identify the speaker. You need both broad and narrow perspectives represented just as you need plot and subplot.

4. **Orderly presentation**. Characters are easier to identify if they generally take turns speaking (whether they would do in real life or not), and dialogue tags (he said and she said) should be used to clarify both speaking out of turn and occasional reminders where the reader might not be sure who is speaking in a long run of speeches or an during unexpected turn of events. The grammar rule of employing nouns before pronouns should be observed.

5. **Subtle presentation**. Descriptive tags other than "said" should be rare and only employed when the reader might have reason to think that a line would have been spoken differently than the reader has reason to expect from the context of the situation and what is being said.

6. **Action tags**. The companion to a dialogue tag is the action tag and this can occasionally be used to match a speaker's action accompanying dialogue to help identify the person while providing a natural flow of events around the conversation. (Example: "I tell you it can be done," said the Colonel, pulling out his

snuff box for a quick sneeze.) The action could also come in advance of the dialogue and include the character's name, in which case you need not further identify the speaker.

Verbal Gimmicks

Verbal gimmicks, such as verbal ticks, common sayings, distinctive speech patterns, and accents have their place in dialogue as well, when used in proper moderation, so by all means use them *after* you have considered the effects of all of the larger drivers. Accents should be limited to a small sample followed by a further description or two in place of verbatim transliteration, as they can become surprisingly tedious. For example, for a Southern U.S. accent you can keep the "y'all" if necessary, but don't lead your reader on a leash by misspelling every word in an attempt to be true to the accent. The constant misspelling approach has rarely worked and in any case is not considered a modern tool of writing because the modern reader doesn't want to wade through it. In Stephen King's 2015 novel *Revival*, he illustrates accented and unusual speech patterns only for minor characters whose job it is to deliver a single short speech.

The bottom line is that you have to understand your "actors." You don't simply *decide* how a character speaks; you decide how that character *would* speak, just as you don't really *decide* what the character will do in any given circumstance so much as discover what his unique combination of traits suggest about what he would do

For a discussion of inadvisable dialogue content, see the section on Exposition.

Dialogue Tags

Dialogue tags are the labels that show who is speaking and sometimes how they are speaking. You don't want to throw a lot of junk in tags because you want to help, not hinder, the smooth flow of the story. In order of highest to lowest frequency, good dialogue tags consist of:

1. **None at all**. It is not necessary to constantly label who is talking. If there are only two people conversing with each other, and their characteristics and roles are well established, then the reader will generally be able to follow the interplay under the assumption that characters take turns speaking whenever they see a new set of quotes in a new paragraph.

2. **Use of the word "said,"** either preceding or following your dialogue. This tag goes with their name, when it's necessary, or a pronoun if the name has already been established and remains clear. Less often, the tag "said," with

the character's name or title is used to insert a dramatic pause in the middle of a statement or to emphasize from which authority they speak. An example of the latter is using their professional title in support of related dialogue.

3. **Use of a tag mixed with an action** in order to enhance visualization of the scene. The action may or may not be part of the same sentence with the tag.

4. **Use of a tag other than "said"** when it is necessary to point out that it was said in a special way.

For **Exercise D1**, imagine characters A and B (give them names before you begin), who are married to each other, having an argument. Use as many of the above dialogue drivers and techniques as possible to assign speech patterns to each. Create two columns on a sheet and use the left half of the page for pure dialogue and the other half to include dialogue tags.

For **Exercise D2**, characters A and B are the same people but do not know each other. Character A will sell a car to character B.

Chapter Eight

A Beginning Well Made

Focus on the Start

There is no way to overestimate the importance of the opening pages of a story and the time you must spend on it. This is where you either draw the reader in, or your book is abandoned and forgotten like a weak Spartan child. The beginning is necessarily a rocky place that can make all of your effort in crafting the story come to nothing. Here the author faces every disadvantage:

1. No one knows your character.

2. No one cares.

3. The author feels under pressure to include a great deal of background information simultaneously in order to convey the plot or at least some larger context. And you can't do that.

If the piece represents a subsequent volume in a series, the character and the situation must be re-introduced to make up for the likely interval between reading one volume and the next. But there is no chance of a next volume unless you spend longer on decisions concerning the beginning—and the rewriting of the beginning—than any other part. Many professional authors experience ongoing difficulty producing the ideal opening. You will too.

Entering the Timeline

For most genres, the best advice was always: Start the tale as near to the end of the story as possible. Prefer a story span of hours, days, or weeks over months or years. **The exciting parts are near the end; don't drag us through the dull.** Do not confuse the entry point of the story for the reader with the possible beginning point of your writing, known as the key scene, which may be buried anywhere in story; we are speaking here of what the reader sees on Page One.

That said, placement of the starting line depends largely on how much room you have to tell your story.

If it is an "epic," intended to span a lifetime or whole generations and the book will be thick or part of a set of many volumes, then the long time span belongs in the story because intervening events will be illustrated. Even in that case, you must treat each of the smaller component tales as stories that begin near their ending.

If overall space is relatively short (a single novel's length or less) and you've conceived a story where your earlier and later events are widely scattered, then you are forced to create one or more large, potentially distracting or disappointing gaps, and make some awkward decisions about how to handle those gaps. The more your reader loves your story, the more she hates wondering about the omitted intervals. Start your tale near the end of the story.

Choosing the Opening Scene

A scene is a single, coherent and unbroken sequence that could be explained in terms of its identifiable function in a story, e.g.:

- Janice went for a drive and saw something she wasn't intended to see.
- Roland had a dream that helped him come to grips with his situation (or frightened him more).
- Bergen went to a supermarket and ran into a previous lover with whom he might rekindle an affair.
- Dottie came across a piece of real estate that would turn out to be a haunted house.

- Greco found crumbs on the table each morning and came to the realization that he'd been sleep-eating.

Remembering that we are starting near the end, begin with an inciting event, the last big one, the one that starts the boulder rolling down the hill, or the one that changes the direction of a boulder already rolling. The incident may be revealed as late as the end of the first chapter as long as the first chapter is a single scene. To know if you are in the right place, you must be able to answer the questions:

1. Why does my story start here?

2. And why doesn't it start somewhere else?

These are two distinct questions because you may have a reason for starting at one point, but the second question makes you realize there was a better solution.

Exercise B1 (regarding the beginning): You must get a sense of what a scene should be before you choose your opening scene. Pick a scene suggestion from the list above and turn it into a real scene with details, several paragraphs long. Make sure that the qualities of the characters and their environment are apparent (at the very least) and make sure you accomplish what the scene is designed to accomplish. Don't worry that you don't know everything. You will revisit this scene list after you have studied other story elements, but that is no reason not to get started now.

7 Brilliant Ways to Start

What do various authors do to get over the fact that they need to tell a story while no one knows their characters, no one knows the situation, and no one cares? Here are several opening strategies that cover almost every novel on the shelves:

1. **The inciting incident appears to be small and simple** but will turn out to be the first step in a chain reaction that forms the story arc for the entire book. In Irving A. Greenfield's Ancient *of Days*, a primitive hunter encounters a hungry old man while he is trying to bring down a bear. The hungry old man, who he grudgingly feeds, turns out to be a messenger from God who sends our hero down the path that leads him to direct the building of Stonehenge. Meanwhile, we are drawn into the story while worrying only about the scope of a stand-off over some meat. How the hero handles himself tells us that he is a great hunter among a starving, self-reliant people, and he is nonetheless capable of learning compassion, which is the simultaneous characterization that makes the reader care.

2. **Do the opposite: start with a moment so consequential that it cannot be ignored.** This may or not lead to a flashback, but do not cheat

with a false opening that is only an attention getter. In Dean Koontz' *The Vision*, we immediately start with a psychic describing a gory murder. After a page and a half of this we get the context. The opening is legitimate because she will really turn out to be psychic and will be in the center of it all.

3. Start with **a lifestyle that is so unusual** in its illustration that most readers are interested because they are unfamiliar with the culture, custom or practice. Perhaps they know of it but have never known its details. In *Tishamingo Blues*, Elmore Leonard tells the story of a man who makes his living as a carnival-style high diver, and he begins, not with an immediate incident but with a description of how he sells his art by making the danger seem as colorful as possible. Once the author has provided the flavor through the words of his character, he then serves up the inciting incident on the third page. As it turns out, the inciting incident was merely the prospect for a new gig for our hero. Now you know why Leonard did not start with the inciting incident *per se*, but the colorful part just before that. This would be a tough choice to pull off for an author who was not a master of the craft.

4. Make sure that the opening scene does the work of **characterization** by showing action that helps explain the most central aspect of the character. One way to do this is to provide a familiar situation with an engagingly fresh viewpoint. The character you invent has to be extraordinarily interesting. If

you choose this route, though, you had better be right about that assessment. To be safe, the technique is usually combined with another. This method, once chosen, can and must be continued throughout the work. In *Forrest Gump*, the title character, with his professed IQ of 70, tells his own story, opening with, "Let me say this: bein a idiot is no box of chocolates," and then illustrates his troubles with the time a neighbor asks if he wants to make some money. He agrees and is put to brutal physical work for which he is paid only one dollar. He knows he has been cheated but doesn't know how to express it. He emphasizes that idiots tend to know more than people give them credit for. Before the first chapter is over, we know that our hero is a man who looks at the fundamentals of life. In the movie version, which must immediately establish a sense of his adventures to come, the opening sequence follows a feather caught in updrafts and being gently buffeted far and wide until it finds him at a bus stop bench where he will soon repeat the "box of chocolates" comment in the context of "you never know what you're gonna get." From this vignette—the one chosen to introduce the character in commercials—we see that the character is pleased with the idea that none of us know what the adventure will hold. His outlook carries a positive fate for him on a current that sweeps right past his simplicity. So the essence of the whole story is right there.

5. Start with a **prologue** that might be labeled as such for a whole chapter length, or might be only an

unlabeled paragraph that serves the same purpose, or anything in between. The prologue describes an earlier situation or fact upon which the whole story is based. Sara Shepard's novel *Flawless*, in the *Pretty Little Liars* series, starts with a stand-alone paragraph that identifies and explains a particular "black cat boy," a stalker who brings bad luck whenever he crosses your path, and we're told that "every town has one." In the following scene, it describes a girls-only party that the black cat boy interrupts, which leads immediately to our heroes wanting to get even with him, and the disaster that follows their revenge. The foundational situation may also be presented without any apparent prologue as in the case of a very powerful opening by James Leo Herlihy in his 1960 novel *All Fall Down*. Here too is a case where every town has one—"a house that is special." He then tells us the various reasons that a house could be special. From there he focuses on a particular house and then the rumors and then the reasons for the rumors. Before you know it, we are deep into listening to this story. The reader is given no pause to even consider whether or not they will read it all. Some authors say you must *never* use a prologue if you wish to be successful. Try telling that to fans of Dan Brown (*The DaVinci Code*) or fans of Stieg Larsson (*The Girl with the Dragon Tattoo*). The prologue is alive and flourishing. Of course, if you as an author don't handle it well, then don't use it until you have read books with effective prologues in them. The most effective prologues are those of the "whole story is based on it" variety, not the ones that are just a throwaway, placed there for color.

6. **Prologue variant—the memory**. Stephen King does this better than anyone in his novel *Thinner*, where a character's memory of an event is italicized. For the recollection, King uses present tense to summon immediacy before switching to past tense, which is actually the present action of the story! The tale literally begins with the title word "thinner," as dialog, and then describes how the gypsy laid on his curse with vivid physical detail. Our hero is shown to be experiencing the memory because he is currently in the act of weighing himself and he has indeed lost a few pounds, an event he attempts to take lightly despite the curse in the very near background. He relentlessly returns to a state of fear by page three and the intensity of the story never lets up.

7. *In medias res*, which is Latin for "in the midst of things." This is a narrative technique that catches attention by rather abruptly starting with a major incident in progress or almost so. In *Water for Elephants*, Sara Gruen uses a prologue where it briefly appears as if she is simply describing life in a circus for a new recruit. Then, in a lively three-page sequence, the animals break loose and our hero tries to help and witnesses someone committing a murder during the chaos. At the start of the next chapter, however, the first-person narrative describes what it is like to be a nonagenarian in a nursing home, an experience that is as unfamiliar to most readers as life in a circus. (Elmore Leonard, in

all his rich versatility, uses this technique as well in his novel *Touch*, which begins with the extremely violent temper tantrum of a drunk).

Exercise B2: Choose a scene from the strategy list above, making sure it's from a book that you haven't read yet. Considering the entire context, but not necessarily including it all, write your version of the opening scene.

Crafting the Opening Chapter

While the opening scene itself is most important, a scene is usually not the same thing as a chapter. Most chapters are a collection of scenes that have been gathered together for a reason. Subject them to a similar, but larger analysis than the one you do for scenes. For all chapters, ask yourself if you could explain the purpose of the chapter, and why anyone would feel impelled to continue reading the book when they finish any particular chapter, especially Chapter One.

The chapter boundary should appear to be a natural stopping point (if you craft it so), but its end should be so intriguing that it would be painful for the reader not to begin the next chapter immediately. This procedure is especially critical for the first chapter. All of the novels mentioned above begin to explain the intriguing background of the situation after one or two pages. They give just enough for the reader to feel that they *haven't* heard enough (See Exposition Done Right).

Chapter Nine

Exposition Done Right

The general rule for all aspects of writing is, "show, don't tell," one of the most misunderstood instructions ever to disgrace an English class. The controversy about exposition's role in "show, don't tell" arises in the context of revealing information about setting, character description, cultural details, dialogue, and plot support. Exposition, in the narrative sense, refers to any part of the story where important background information is introduced. That doesn't mean that exposition equals "tell."

The problem comes when writing students acquire the perception that exposition (or background information) is evil. Out of this fear, they over-broaden the definition to include the provision of all information, and then reject the idea of using exposition anywhere at any time.

The "show don't tell" directive simply means that you must never forget that entertainment is at the heart of all storytelling. Of course you are *telling* and of course you are directly explaining sometimes; a book is not a movie and even in a movie you are directly explaining sometimes. **But the process must seem to the reader *as if you are showing*,** and you must do that well enough that you engage the reader's visual cortex at least some of the time. What you don't want is for telling to sound like lecturing. Windy explanations are highly accurate and rarely entertaining. If a complex idea is critical to the plot—as often comes up in science fiction—you simplify the concept and break it down into digestible pieces by illustrating its parts and having the characters question each part. Be stingy with your explanations because there will always be another opportunity later to tell more. So forget about the old formula. The less-concise truth is:

Show and Tell *Well*, Don't Lecture

Once you shed the pedantic, professorial mode, you go to the next step and make sure you are not summarizing. Summarizing actions or events has its place (and we'll get to that later), but explaining too briefly is the second level of what exposes this feeling of being "told" something. The reader has a hard time visualizing that which is not laid out in detail. When they can just about visualize what you are saying if they squint hard enough, they are still not happy. Readers don't want to feel like they are telling the story to themselves. And that leads us to the next truth:

When You Show, it's Blow by Blow

That doesn't mean you eliminate exposition to get it out of the way! It means that you learn to do it right. A broad definition of exposition can actually be useful because you need to know how to handle the distribution of all of your story information in the most profitable way. We will allow that exposition includes at least all *relevant* information.

Tools of Exposition

1. **Content**. In writing the classic newspaper article it is a virtue to present raw facts in the spectrum of "who, what, when, why, where, and how." In storytelling you must do no less! You need to eventually provide those same "five w's and an "h," but embellishment and style count heavily, and the presentation sequence is entirely different from the journalistic approach.

2. **Timing**. Exposition—or direct explanation of a concept or its background—should occur naturally throughout the book, as needed, and never occur outside of what is needed. Otherwise you have what is perceived as an "info dump," a foible well parodied by the character named Basil Exposition in the Austin Powers film series. If instead your explanations read like a great meal's side dish and come when the reader is hungry for them, the fare will *never* taste like lecturing.

Example of an exposition sequence: (A) Cole watched Myra remove all of the books from her shelves and replace them one by one, in category order rather than her usual alphabetical arrangement. (B) When she was done, Cole put his arm around her shoulder and drew her close. (C) Poor Myra only rearranged books when she was distraught.

The last line here can be considered exposition, something you would only want to know about if an action relevant to the information is happening *right now*, and it *is*. You might then go on to tell us of the history of her habit or of how her friend knows about it, but that depends on which part of the book we are in (see Exposition in the big picture, below) and how important it is for the reader to know these larger facts.

Suggestion:
Habitually put a relevant action before exposition.

Otherwise you are offering an explanation in support of nothing. Consider how the above example would have been weakened if Sentence C had been Sentence A.

Exposition in Dialogue: The Special Case

No discussion about exposition is complete without examining the case of "as you know, Bob," also known as "the idiot lecture." The common misconception of the semi-professional writer is that characters must never smuggle exposition into a story under cover of quote marks. Yes and no. The "rule" is not so pat. The same folk will also tell you that they "learned" in a very respectable writing class that ALL exposition is an inherent vice, and the need to shun it is why ANY explanation is especially outrageous when placed in dialogue. But no one has told them anything of the kind. They simply misunderstood their teacher. **Exposition is not evil. Neither is it disgraceful or even regrettable. It is an essential tool that can be used well or poorly.** The audience wants to know what is going on and they thrive on exposition in the proper place and in the proper dosage. When Sherlock Holmes solves the case, there had damned well better be exposition. And where is that exposition found? In dialogue!

This so-called dialogue dump works perfectly for Sherlock because is informing people who are not as smart as he is. NO ONE is as smart as he is so we don't feel badly about this.

There are cases where Bob should *not* be told things he already knows, but there are also many cases where this method will actually work. The classic method of divulging such information to the audience is where Bill is striving to show Bob what he has learned as they are about to go on a mission, as in, "Let's go over this again, Bill. Prove to me that you know it." But there are other natural ways where people might discuss that which they are already supposed to know.

Example of inept use of exposition

Mary sniffled as she said goodbye to her house. Mary was a violet-eyed girl who loved kittens. (Bad writers have an obsession with violet eyes, but that's beside the point)

And this version isn't much better

Mary locked herself in the dark closet and wiped her bright violet eyes. (Who is looking at her? Tell us about her eye color when it matters to the plot or when a third party cares so that it doesn't seem so forced.)

Try This

Mary locked herself in the Gulf station restroom, took a ragged breath, checked the cracked mirror and, to her horror, saw on brown eye, and one blue: her contact lens had fallen out and now someone was bound to recognize her.

Exposition in the Big Picture

Even when you are an expert in doling out minor exposition such as eye color you still need to know which parts of the plot are most favorable for answering the big questions. Of the total amount of exposition found in novels, the most common distribution appears to be:

1. Beginning – 50-60% (background)

2. Middle – 15-25% (explanation of ongoing efforts)

3. Ending – 20-30% explanations supporting the denouement or aftermath)

That may seem like an awful lot at each and every stage, but remember, the information has to go somewhere, and it all must add up to 100%.

Chapter Ten

Never Soft in the Middle

Real life is not easy. Stories about easy lives do nothing for you as an artist or as an audience because verisimilitude demands that a story reflect some of the complexity of real life. Simplicity brings little in the way of challenges to solve to say nothing of the sweet victories that would follow their resolution. Therefore you must flood the middle section of your novel with worsening conflict formed out of goals and opposition to those goals. Further consider using a series of minor victories amidst erosion of the hero's resources and/ or remaining time to solve the problem. If you choose the latter case, you still need to devise a climax as described below.

Exactly which page numbers, or percentage of pages, mark the exact location or span of your story's middle, no one can say. **The start of your middle** can be thought of as where the set-up has ended and the "adventure" begins. Even when you think you have chosen the spot, analysts will have differing opinions on where they think you have put it. Most readers will recognize the start of the middle as the point where they have really "gotten into" the story, which means that they don't want to stop reading. By then you will have assembled and demonstrated sufficient plot elements to engage an audience, making them say, "That's interesting. I wonder how a story like this will play out for the people involved."

From there, the middle usually consists of:

ATTEMPT – OPPOSITION – FAILURE – REPEAT WITH GREATER FAILURE

In between failures, you may wish to place small, costly victories. Exhausting the protagonist also adds to the hurdles of rising action.

The end of the middle corresponds to the so-called **climax**, which is meant to be the point of highest tension, or drama, so far. In a "happy ending" story—the most common variety—the highest drama is where the hero is in the worst position possible. If you know the boundaries of your story, you can plan the climax accordingly. The parameters of a well-made climax are these:

1. **It is hard to imagine** how anything can ever be right again.

2. **If it were easy to imagine**, then there would be no point in reading further.

3. **If you make it impossible to imagine** the resolution, then you will have an unsatisfying resolution or none at all.

The Sum of All Strengths

As you fight your way through mid-book—the planning and the execution both—and wonder sometimes at your choices, remember that every writer makes errors. Every blessed one of them. With the great authors you may never notice it, and you certainly would not know that the story fell short of what the writer intended it to be. With top-level contemporary authors, the reader quickly forgives and forgets the errors as they come. There is a solid reason for that.

As long as we do more things right than wrong, we writers are perceived as the sum of all of our strengths.

The reality is that this strength weighting is net of our weaknesses, but these faults are subsumed by the dramatic process known as "suspension of disbelief." Unaware of the dynamics of relative strength, we will sometimes replicate the errors of great writers, mistakenly thinking that they can do no wrong.

You avoid the problem of error copying as best you can by being aware of its existence on every author's plate. For example, in Stieg Larsson's *The Girl with the Dragon Tattoo*, chapter 7 begins with a conversation between Erika Berger and Mikael Blomkvist. On the second page, we find out that not only is there a third person in the room with them, but that the chapter is *his* POV. Since Christer Malm is not part of the conversation until the end, and we only hear one of his thoughts early on, it never becomes clear why it should have been his POV.

To a novice writer (let's say someone who has written two or fewer novels), it's cool and exciting that a pro has done something unconventional, and the novice wants to try it out. But the pro in this case has simply made a mistake (an irritating one at that) and gotten away with it in the bigger context of an otherwise excellent novel. In Chapter 11, he makes an even more obvious mistake, switching the POV in the very last paragraph, but his characterization is spectacular. The novice will probably not get away with the same error, and even if you do, it will only serve to weaken your novel, not strengthen it.

How do you know mistake from genius? Herein lies the role of experience. I suggest you take into consideration the following clues:

1. Did the technique take you by surprise and cause you to change your perception? If so, that is not a good sign.

2. Did you have a hard time seeing the purpose of the technique? If the answer is yes, then it was

probably a patch, an inferior solution to a problem that the author experienced in relating his narrative.

3. If both answers are yes, then you can be sure that whatever was done could have been done better.

Getting back to *The Girl with the Dragon Tattoo*, in chapter 7, even though Christer Malm finally enters the conversation at the end of the scene and helps settle the matter of Blomkvist taking the new job, we don't get any of this thought process on this subject. The discussion itself is quite solid and entirely necessary, but the POV choice is clearly a half-formed idea, possibly the result of last minute advice to keep Malm from being a complete non-entity.

Let's take a look at how Larsson could have done his chapter 7 better, even *with* the questionable POV choice:

First of all, he could have eliminated the initial confusion by letting us know that it was Christer Malm's POV at the start. That would cost nothing.

Second, he could have taken more of an opportunity to shed light on Berger and Blomkvist through his third party perspective as they spoke (the opportunity is barely touched upon). Just because their characters are well covered elsewhere does not mean you should avoid characterization where you would expect to find it.

And third, he could have shared the impulse that finally spurred Malm to speak up. That would normally be the purpose of using a lesser character's POV.

The bottom line is that those who consistently produce best-selling books have the chops get away with many of the flaws that lesser writers cannot. They often do so by providing the best possible wallpaper to cover ill-conceived plot devices (a much bigger mistake than one chapter's POV), and follow it up with stunning high-emotion craftsmanship once we arrive at the forced scene, thus convincing us of the situation's "rightness" no matter how we got there. Exhibit brilliance and take a bow.

Chapter Eleven

The Ending You So Richly Deserve

The ending of a novel demonstrates how everything works out, usually drawing in all (or enough of) the plot threads the author has sprinkled about so that the picture finally "makes sense." Readers will love you if you make your ending satisfying. Satisfaction tends to come from these elements:

1. **Reader logic.** A measurement of how much the story makes sense, which comes from the answers to these two questions:

    a. Did you build the ending out of existing materials or did you suddenly introduce unfamiliar ideas? Consistency goes to the author's **perceived level of honesty**. Material that we haven't gotten a chance to live with *feels* less honest because it leaves the reader in the cold; and

    b. Did the resolution illuminate some **rule of human nature**? E.g. "people want what they can't have," or "be careful what you wish for," or "if you build it, they will come." This principle straddles both logic and gains.

99

2. **Gains.** The **climatic gain** is achievement of the objective. The **falling action gain** is how well our hero achieved a new perspective, separate and apart from any *material* gains. This quality is also known as "growth," and it can be judged with the following criteria:

   a. **Movement**. Is the protagonist standing in a different position as compared to the beginning of the story?

   b. **Understanding the lesson taught by the experience**. For example, has your protagonist found out that getting what you want is impossible? Some of the most popular stories follow the Rolling Stones' formula: "You can't always get what you want, but if you try sometimes, you just might find, you get what you need." This is because desires cannot withstand a firestorm of opposition; only necessities can do that. *The Wizard of Oz*, one of the most popular stories of all time, can easily be accused of anti-climax (see plot, earlier) because the all-powerful wizard is all-bluff. But any perception of anti-climax is amply repaired and forgiven in the context of lessons learned. People getting what they really need always strikes a chord in terms of logic and gain.

100

c. **Purchased achievement and wisdom**. Did our hero pay a significant price (pain, suffering and loss) for the above gains? The answer needs to be yes. Therefore a happy resolution is NOT about winning everything. As songwriter Rihanna, puts it, "What's love without tragedy?"

Chapter Twelve

What about the Sequel?

The first question is: why talk about sequels if you haven't written your first book yet? Because readers and viewers love sequels since they have invested in the characters, along with their world, and authors love sequels for the same reason.

And because, from a practical standpoint, you must consider the possibility of a sequel to your current work because it affects your story structure, demanding a big arc over the smaller arc of individual books. Structural elements that you don't plan for up front often turn out to be exponentially more difficult for you to adjust later.

I'm convinced that most successful sequel authors have forgotten how they've managed it. That is to say, they have internalized the process so well that they can no longer externalize their procedure well enough to teach it.

To be fair, sequels can often be the product of a tortured path and input from multiple sources. Fortunately, we have a vast number of sequels for all to examine and learn from, provided we focus on the building blocks. That would be the types of sequels, what their ingredients are, and how they fit into the big structure.

Types of Sequels

There are only a few basic categories of novel sequels. The rest are hybrids. (When it comes to movies, those have another few wrinkles, such as the reboot that retells and reimagines the whole nature of the story or character, usually in order to milk a franchise or expand something that wasn't a franchise to begin with. Remember that we are focusing on novels here and dipping into movies either because they have followed a novel or because their transferrable lessons are clear.) Terms have been coined for nearly all of the hybrids, but it's not useful to memorize them. The familiar categories can be sorted into these neat piles:

1. **The continuing story.** This includes every quest ever known. Think *Lord of the Rings*, which could have taken any number of books to complete. It also includes what I call the Big Mystery. An undertaking of this kind requires the big story arc that overarches each and every arc that tells the tale within the covers of a single book. For a sample of a sequel built on the Big Mystery, see the appendix to this book.

2. **The new mission.** This can be done with any character whose life consists of missions or cases, such as the military and law enforcement, or private investigation. If you are writing one of these you understand very well that they are a format naturally suited for sequels.

3. **Another generation.** *Son of Frankenstein,* for a clear and ready example. In novels, think of the author Stephen Coonts and how he utilized both techniques 2 and 3 in the same universe. The series he began with *Flight of the Intruder* had each book represent another of Jake Grafton's continuing missions, allowing the character to age in approximately real time until the author picked up with adventures of the next generation. But Coonts didn't restrict himself to the actual offspring of the main character. He dipped into other, younger, characters he had created along the way, which gave the reader continuity. This can also be done a different kind of continuity, as in the series that was actually called *The Next Generation* but was not intended to consist of characters created in the prior *Star Trek* works or their offspring.

Problems with Sequels

The most common problems with novel sequels are these:

1. **The Disconnect.** We can't remember what the author is talking about and don't have enough information to piece it together.

2. **The Painful Recap.** We're told *too* much of the previous story in a way that does not feel like movement and does not seem entertaining.

3. **The Time Gap.** Even when a sequel comes out as soon as the publishing process allows, there will be fans who believe it took too long.

4. **The Wrong Direction.** As far as readers are concerned, the wrong things happened in the sequel. They've had lots of time to think about it.

5. **The dreaded re-hash.** The author has run out of ideas and there seems to be no other place to go with the story. This is mainly an issue found in movies because success of the first film was unforeseen and the sequel is not a product of the original author's imagination. A re-hash can

occasionally happen with books too, as a result of bad planning.

To What Extent Resolved?

In real life, successful people have new problems and a new perspective on life. All it requires is the passage of time. So it is with the best novels.

Orson Scott Card's *Ender's Game,* or the *Ender Saga,* to embrace the whole sweep, is one of the most complicated of sequel series. We won't go into all the ramifications, but suffice to say Card jumps back and forth in the time line, sometimes thousands of years, and revisits the same events from other points of view, which is rarely done, even in the cinema. If an approach is unique, or close to it, it probably shouldn't be listed as a separate category; *Ender's Game* qualifies in all three categories above.

Didn't Live Happily Ever After

Sequels are all about the fact that no matter what it looked like at the end of the last installment, our hero did not really live happily ever after. One day he might, though!

In the hugely successful *Die Hard* movie series, John McClane is happy at the end of each movie, but this is based on the novel *Nothing Lasts Forever*! So far, he has suffered 27 years of misery because none of what he's done has been popular with is family. But he's a man of integrity. He goes on saving their lives anyway. Another day, another mission. That's how you do it.

When Sequels are Prequels

Harper Lee's *To Kill a Mockingbird* was an instant prequel to a book that didn't get published until 2015. This bears some explanation. The original manuscript was in fact its own prequel because the flashbacks were extracted and made into the first book. The newly released manuscript, *Go Set a Watchman*, sometimes billed as a sequel, is the balance of the original, abandoned work. Nonetheless, for our purposes, the tactic of extracting flashbacks and focusing on prequel material illustrates something of the range of brilliant tactics that can be employed to find a new direction for your novel.

Prequels, whether they arise through a conventional process or not, are the reason that it's more correct to say, as we did above, "another generation," rather than next generation. The material could stem from the next generation, the previous generation, or an earlier period in an older character's life, which likely brings in parents of the younger characters from the initial book.

Ingredients of a Sequel

As with all novel writing challenges, the problems of sequels can be solved by awareness and planning, as well as writing experience. Therefore, take a look at what most successful sequels have:

1. **Continuity.** This is a must. Remember that people desire sequels because they've grown enamored with the characters, situations, and style, and/ or authorial voice, of the first book. You must support your continuity in a way that readers will find satisfying (there's that word "satisfying" again!) by supporting the elements of continuity. If not, there is no point to having a sequel. What quantity of ingredients will be enough, is up to the cook.

2. **Fresh Blood.** This is strongly recommended. If you bring in new characters, we can see how the old characters react to them, and not feel like we are reading the same book over again.

3. **Revelation.** Another must. Deeper into the mystery, deeper along the track of life. If you've revealed all the secrets in the first book, you've made a mistake. But perhaps there are things about your character's past that affect the present and have not been explored yet.

4. **Relocation.** This is a maybe. Remove your character from their comfortable surroundings and put them in a completely unfamiliar situation so we can learn about them and their capabilities all over again as they learn about the new situation.

Of course if you have a mission-oriented series most of your task is to simply pick up the new mission.

Exercise S1: Take a new book that you've read (or an old book that never had a sequel) and outline where you would go with it based on one or more of the sequel models above. Do you think the book was built to allow for a sequel or not? If not, can you get past that? Which characters will you pick up, and which threads?

Exercise S2: Choose a book that already has sequels, but you haven't read them. This way you can get (relatively) quick feedback. Make your prediction about what you will find in the sequels, and then check to see how many of your predictions hold up. Try to make substantive and specific predictions based on the situation at the end of the book and the underlying dynamics of the situation over time.

PART II All the Rest

Chapter Thirteen

The Writing Community

How Writing Club Postings Motivate

It's common to write for the pleasure of a single person who serves as your muse, a practice that attunes you to a coherent set of sensibilities instead of finding yourself scattered. Since it is easier to do that than to share your work with other *writers*, one of the most common novice questions is whether you ought to make the effort to share your work on a broader front at all, let alone the people who are in the same boat as you.

The answer is you should share your work with other writers because that way you get more practical responses and suggestions than you do with general readers.

People engaged on similar efforts provide a different and usually more precise perspective on writing or potential publishing issues.

Both kinds of input are essential, however, because non-authors give you a more basic sense of whether you have raw talent that appeals to them.

When we say write for "a person," a small and well-defined audience can serve that purpose. A writing club, properly run—and with their responses to your work properly analyzed and digested by you—may be the very "person" that serves as your tuning fork.

Often found under the heading of "writing communities," you will be amazed at the quality of the writing from the "amateurs" that populate these venues. Be prepared to be a bit intimidated, just in case. Here are a few popular outlets that cater to a full range of genres: Writing.com, WritersCafe.org, Authonomy.com, and Scribophile.com. Critters.org and quantummuse.com are examples of genre specialty sites that cater to science fiction, fantasy and horror.

If you are the friendly type, you will make friends in these venues. Do not expect to make *valuable* writing contacts of the kind that can propel you to the top should you impress them. Such connections could happen, but not any time soon since there are not enough industry people logged in as compared to the large numbers of people vying for attention in the club. In any case, industry people generally don't feel the need to join such a club in order to scout for talent. Don't worry about that. Join a club where you feel a sense of belonging. The feeling of community it brings to your otherwise solitary pursuit is ample reward.

Measuring Writing Club Reviews

Avoid getting stuck: Writing club audiences add to the number of opinions you receive on your work, a resource that might elsewise be completely absent from your process. If you get one or more opinions that you don't like, you will more likely question whether that input is valid than if the reviewer called you brilliant. You don't necessarily have to run and change your work on the strength of a single writing club review with specific criticisms. On the other hand, don't completely discount a suggestion because only one person said it—they may be the very person who represents a key segment of your readership.

If several people say the same thing, that is a strong indicator that they are right no matter what your instinct has told you; if comments conflict or are isolated, remember that you are the author, and the final application of your judgment can only come from you. Sometimes everyone is right in their identification of a problem but wrong in their suggested solution. Experiment with changes that feel right to you and tell your reviewers how much you would appreciate it if they would read the work again. Of course you must do the same thing for them.

The Writing Club Caveat

Note that by placing your work on these sites, you are "publishing" your work in the sense that your work has been made available to the public. Putting something on the Internet, even if only a handful of people read it, is legally no different than having your work printed in the local penny saver. You've produced; you've released; you've made some attempt to disseminate. You are to be congratulated.

But there is, on rare occasion, a downside to seeking reviews and sharing in a community. If there is a mechanism in your club by which non-members cannot view your work, I suggest you utilize that control because invisible non-members may be less scrupulous about respecting your copyright.

Old school publishers, moreover, may be less interested in taking a chance on you if your work has already been read by the fans who will like it. Therefore there is no money at all to be made on your work. At least that is the way they will see it. Keeping your work-in-progress off of the public view setting may be critically important in that sense.

Why Writing Conferences Work

Conferences and book fairs exist all over the United States and in other countries. Some may be convenient to your location while others require travel. You may wish to travel once every five years or you may do it every year. We can tell you right up front:

Information = Motivation

Bringing yourself into contact with writers on many levels is another way of drawing strength and sharing tips from the greater community. There are seminars to be had that examine the writing craft from every angle. Successful people will be there. You may even meet a favorite author. More importantly, sitting in with industry experts who give you a preview of what is ahead in terms of getting an agent or what it's like to make a big sale is akin to adding a spark plug to your work. They mention exciting things like sales numbers and the dollars that go with them. Go and get that invaluable experience.

Chapter Fourteen

The Truth about Words

The Word Count Paradox

Even if you go to conferences for the sole purpose of immersing yourself in marketing techniques, you should never stop writing and measuring your progress on your off-hours. But how do you really measure headway?

The first step in a writer's evolution is to stop talking about how many "pages" you've written, and start talking about word count. Pages mean nothing because they vary according to fonts, font sizes, margins and line spacing. Word count is a universal measure for agents and editors, the people who matter when the manuscript leaves your hands. Word count is also a common motivator that brings a sense of community to your writing life.

But the second, and ultimately more important step in a healthy evolution, is to then STOP boasting about word-count alone! All of those words you've piled to the sky may be garbage.

Try reformulating your thinking to:

This is how many new words I've written today, and here is the volume of work I've *self-edited*.

You can also tally the number of plot points you've worked out or how much you've outlined. Any of these metrics are comparable to what you've accomplished on a previous day. When you realize that writing is more than stacking words, then you will finally have useful measurements of your progress.

Don't Slow Down for Grammar Police

Many members of the Grammar Police—those who demand your adherence to everything they've ever learned or thought they learned—troll both online and in-person writing clubs. Some of them have all kinds of impressive-sounding credentials. Most of them, far from seeing themselves as troll-ish, believe they are doing a great public service, usually because they don't know how to do a proper job of non-grammar criticism (and many of them will admit that). None of that matters. You—writer—are not in the business of being a grammarian. That's the beauty of writing prose in the real world. Learn your grammar first-hand (really learn it) and then do what feels right in a particular situation. If someone wants to tell you differently, remind yourself of those who broke the rules and will never be forgotten for their brilliance: Mark Twain, Charles Dickens, Elmore Leonard, etc.

Does that mean that if you break rules, *you* are Twain and Dickens? No. There are certain standards beyond which they did not fall, you do not wish to fall.

I will give you three rules in this arena to avoid grief:

Rule # 1: Some of the conventions of grammar, such as parallelism, or the past perfect tense, exist for the sake of clarity. Almost always, it is not your intention to be unclear. You have a story to tell and you want your readers to understand every moment of it whenever possible, so these conventions are indispensable. If you know your grammar, you know which rules are necessary and which are unnecessary regardless of the narrative form and aspect you are employing. **Clarity is king**.

Rule # 2: If you are working with first person narration and the ideas you want to get across would **sound right 364 days of the year** when you hear them in conversation, raise the level one notch (with the addition of clarifying words), and you're fine.

Rule # 3: If you are crafting a line of dialogue, **go by what your character would say**. If it drives you crazy to say it wrong, then it must not fit the character you are creating. Also, there is a limit as to how much tortured English the reader can endure, so you want to curtail the distorted output of a character who is incomprehensible.

Last Resort, Write Poorly!

Before you write well, you are obliged to write poorly or not write at all.

At some point you must simply learn to finish, i.e. complete a story, a quality of increasing importance in the modern world. Too many people refuse to wrap up a story and move on due to a false sense that they are a perfectionist and this is how the highest of quality happens. Instead of perfecting the story, though, they leave it unfinished and wonder how it will get done. The answer is that it won't. The most fearful of procrastinators believe that in leaving their work open ended they are avoiding making their failure official. But perfecting your work does not happen outside of the fullness of experience that comes from finishing a draft and then revising that draft. Or by moving on and then coming back to revise earlier work. Fear of producing bad work will produce no work. As Dr. Seuss, the most accomplished children's author of all time, liked to remind us, "Everything stinks till it's finished."

On another place on the literary spectrum, extraordinary wordsmith Stephen King was brave enough to reveal that his first own drafts are terrible (and they truly are). If you've never read Stephen King, his final manuscripts contain some of the finest prose to be found anywhere.

Finishing your work "badly" and then fixing it under my Hammer Method (see below), beats the limited productivity of a misguided perfectionist streak every time. Break those eggs or you may never see that omelet!

Note that this advice is *not* intended for those who currently write volumes of poorly worded text. Those writers have already gone overboard in this direction, practicing their art in a dysfunctional manner rather than writing poorly as a breakout exercise. Remember, we said at the beginning that you need to know which kind of writer you are. The idea of writing badly in order to get something done and something to noodle over is primarily for the Builder category, those who have their toes in the water and need immersion. Destroyers occasionally need it too, but must use it more sparingly.

Chapter Fifteen

Let's Get Finished

Live Inside its Pages

Day and night, you must live the lives of your characters to see what they will do next. That means you must project your mind into the same situations and face the same questions as your heroes and villains, *as if their challenges are your personal issues.*

Solving your character's problems is a highly consuming and rewarding task. The objective is to move the stubborn parts along and do it in a realistic way. The approach is an extremely common one for authors who produce realistic material at length. For example, when I edited the re-print of the bestseller *Ancient of Days: The Chronicles of Ronstrom the Builder* (by Irving A. Greenfield, author of 300 books), his dedication inscription was: *To Anita, Rick and Nat for being there when I was with Ronstrom.* That should tell you volumes about his devotion to the story. But I've heard versions of this sentiment from just about every successful novel writer I have ever surveyed. And even those who don't pursue this exercise consciously, do it

125

unconsciously while getting on with the other tasks of life.

If you find such an approach abhorrent, that's fine. It means you are probably not a novel writer, but rather some other type of author. Lots of otherwise successful authors are not novel writers and you had best find out about this limitation sooner rather than later.

The Hammer Method

Sometimes the inspiration won't come to you directly, yet you have to get something done, and you need an alternative approach. You may need what I call my Hammer Method. I also call it the Hammer and Anvil Method because there has to be a strike plate, and that refers to your starting point, whatever that might be.

Craftsmen have known for millennia that you can get subtle and exquisite artistic results simply by using a hammer on metal with repeated blows—often employing hundreds of these strikes—in close proximity. The first impacts unsurprisingly start out rough given what appears to be a crude instrument until you bring the necessary heat. Hit the metal as many times as you have to and take as long as you need. When such a course of action becomes necessary, you can do the same for a book.

How it works:

1. Sketch out a scene that you have been having trouble with and then print out the pages no matter how little you have so far or how rough the material is. Throw in every little scrap you have. You need not write poorly on purpose but proceed at top speed so that you can capture any fleeting thoughts you may experience.

2. Go for a long walk (or drive if necessary) and sit down away from home with your print out to read what you have. Mark it up extravagantly with every alteration that brings it into order as well as notes on any wandering thought that comes to mind. Write everywhere and use arrows. If you are not immediately ready to do this, read a few paragraphs of a favorite book first.

3. Take those changes back to your computer (while you can still interpret the sprawl) whereupon you should naturally think of still more improvements to input as you translate your handwritten notes into print. Even the tiniest corrections count because one will lead to another.

4. Now print it out in a different font style and size.

5. When you put yourself back in motion on your next walk (immediately, if possible) where you read it again, some of the blockages that kept you from fleshing out the scene in the first place will be cleared.

6. Repeat, repeat, repeat like the hammer that softens and shapes the metal. Your strike plate—that which supports your effort—is your prior experience; the backing firms up more each time.

The attitude behind this method is that you don't stop for writer's block. You meet the challenge head on. You don't go lie down to grow a Rip Van Winkle beard until the day you feel like an author again. The Hammer Method works for both Builders and Destroyers. Geniuses don't need it.

The Last Word

When you have learned and applied these rules, writing a novel will still be sweat stained, red-eyed honest work. You may meet revision with dread or you may be delighted when you catch each and every mistake that the world at large need never see. To others you may look like a manic depressive, soaring with the acquisition of each new idea, and plummeting when your work grinds to a halt. And you may be as wrung out as you look. Did you think the result would be otherwise?

The difference between the beginning of your study of writing and the point where you finish your first book is that the set of tasks involved will no longer be impossible for you, while tackling those same tasks will remain impossible for others.

Not everyone can write a novel. Whether you become another Hemingway or not, climbing that mountain still ranks high on the human accomplishment scale. That's why novels are valuable, and the challenge itself may be part of the reason you want to write one so badly.

Now finish one novel and write another because (*and here comes an industry secret...*):

History shows that authors, on average, write
SEVEN books
before their first one is traditionally published
or becomes successful as a self-published work.

Since that's only an average,
maybe you will do better!

And while you're thinking about that, start your
next book.

Appendix: Sample Sequel Chapter

The following excerpt is an example of sequel overlap, and this chapter in particular fills in a story gap near the end of the first novel. It ends by intersecting with the first novel events from a different point of view.

CHAPTER 3: This Vessel of Flesh

(From *Kreindia of Amorium*, Upcoming Sequel to *Wade of Aquitaine* by Ben Parris)

"A thousand years in Your sight are but as yesterday"
(Psalm 90:4)

The horror began before Kreindia opened her eyes. A second mind crowded the confines of her skull, manifesting at first in a throbbing pressure, an otherness sharing and dividing, surrounding and smothering. She wasn't privy to the other's thoughts, a vague, primitive wash. They resonated and rippled, turned, struggled and ran aground like a hull scraping rock. Kreindia jostled and asserted, screamed inward and let a storm flare out, feeling her countenance crinkle and flatten against bone in gross reflection of her internal flexing.

Finding a path, the Second darted free, sought a corner and shrank to quiescence, retreating through millions of years of evolution, down and down to the lizard brain, where it lodged. It seemed the Second could go nowhere else. The general's niece would have to endure its presence.

The situation worsened when Kreindia regained her sight in a large box flooded with an unnatural bluish glow. She found herself sitting in dreamy paralysis, arms and legs denying her will, feet, hands, neck, and vocal cords likewise useless. She had materialized in the wrong place with no means of escape.

What she would have told her legs was to lift her from the chair. What she would have told her arms was to pound the walls that hemmed her in. And what she would have bid her neck was to raise her head and scream. Instead she moaned like a dog twitching through a nightmare, and that unintelligible sound frightened her more.

Kreindia's eyes tracked right and left like a narcoleptic buried alive awaiting the last clump of dirt. That minor freedom of movement, however, gave her bad news some detail. A man and woman each dressed in black and white stood to either side of her, a placement reminiscent of palace guards.

After a glance at Kreindia, the two at her sides regarded each other in a fleeting clash. When the woman shrank in self-loathing, the man offered her a cruel smile with lips as thin as any Kreindia had ever seen. In a face that must have been nearly handsome once, his pebble eyes were splashed in red and seemed to have recessed from a lifetime of asking for trouble and getting it. His head was hairless but for grizzled brows and a bit of similarly peppered stubble. Not otherwise plagued by wrinkles, twin wattles of flesh traced his Adam's apple, making his age as much a puzzle as his unbridled hostility toward his companion.

Kreindia wondered if the presence of the pair meant she faced a threat more potent than the trap of her body and the trap of the box. No matter how the fear clamped down on Kreindia's gut she could not rouse her muscles to stand and bolt. Though she cried out for Wade, no more than her dog moan escaped her throat. Could this be Hades? Did the devil possess this surfeit of imagination?

The general's niece could not be governed by fear. If it were not Hades, there had to be a solution amenable even to her reduced circumstances. Wade would not have sent her to this location of his own volition.

Despite her restrictions and the close air that conspired to throttle her, a shapeless something nagged, awakened from the presence of the man. He had robbed her of something vital. She felt she had possessed a hint of the answers she sought just a moment ago. She'd known more than that just two precious moments ago on the astral plane. Another glance at the man clouded her thoughts further and she decided her separation from Wade might account for her unease. The Aquitanian stood alone as well, and his potential course of action worried her.

"You didn't press the damn button," the man said.

Kreindia saw that indeed the wall held a set of button-like discs with thick black numbers on them. If the tableau were meant for use in divination, Kreindia had never seen the method. Furthermore, the buttons had not been holed for sewing and she had no idea why someone would press one.

The woman poked at one of the numbered surfaces and a tiny lamp awoke inside it. At the same time came a small jolt and a sense of movement. Downward? Unless there were men outside with levers, Kreindia's sense of direction must have been utterly useless. These numerologists or diviners did not seem alarmed that they might be lowered into the ground.

Along with the buttons, the astral traveler saw unfamiliar writing on the wall. It shifted in and out of focus at the edge of understanding. Under better circumstances she would have enjoyed the opportunity to decipher it.

The man said, "My family consists of two idiot women."

After another small jolt and a pause, the box cracked. Though no one on either side appeared to have pulled or pried at the vertical lid, it slid in two directions, like a puzzle made to collapse upon itself in hollow layers.

"Kreindel, let's go," the man barked.

*Krein*del *rather than Kreindia?* This then was the girl's body to which she had once before been summoned. Now the general's niece had some idea of where she was, and why another mind resided in the same skull. Kreindia realized that she was the guest and the other the host. She sat in a horse-bereft chariot peering out of the eyes of the girl Kreindel, who she thought of as Del. It explained the sensation of being bound into an immobilizing form-fitting cage but for some imperfect movement above her shoulders and in her hand. For the most part, this vessel of flesh could not move. Kreindia could no more explain this summoning than she could the last brief time it had happened. The current arrangement felt far more permanent as she had not settled so deep before.

Fortunately, she could compel the finger that controlled the tiny magic wand. She pushed it forward like the world's smallest lever and her chariot lurched ahead, passing through the opening with a small bump, and into a corridor beyond.

"To the left, you dolt. You've been here before. How do you get stupider every day? You'd like me to believe the doctor's diagnosis of hysterical paralysis, wouldn't you?"

Kreindia could take little solace in being free of the diviner's box when she remained a captive in every other way. Her female jailer said nothing. In fact she tried to stay out of sight to the rear, but Kreindia got a glimpse of her as she swung the chariot around, and another as she straightened out. Much younger than the man, the woman retained a plain beauty beneath some blemishes on her cheeks and chin. Few locks escaped her pulled back dark brown hair, which was shot through with light streaks above her widow's peak. Her eyes seemed gray one moment and muddy blue the next as though they didn't dare decide what color to be. Her eyebrows had been frightened away entirely. The tip of her nose flared with a ruby shine against fair skin and one cheek was patched red in the shape of a large hand. This was a fellow slave.

They passed into sunlight and through a remarkable translucent door that reminded Kreindia of the brittle substance she had seen Wade crash through in a vision. Birdsong shared the air with an unfamiliar rushing sound. As she listened, the horrible man beside her struck a smarting blow to her head saying, "Look where you're going." She found her thwarted impulse to strike back added to a growing store of anger, and the resolve to find a way out.

In the open air, a machine raced by without benefit of mules, as though demon impelled, with a roar and a foul odor. A long shadow sped alongside in the minutes before sunset. She gaped after it in astonishment.

When she put herself back in motion, the other mind in her skull opened up and she found herself drawn to it in a trickle of commingling. With it came the tantalizing gift of knowledge.

I'm sharing, it said. *To keep us sane*, it said.

Us.

Based on that entreaty, and knowing the other's identity now, Kreindia cooperated. What began as a gentle tug enveloped her and then seized her like the madness she'd hoped to avoid. Too late she realized it was lunacy to abandon one mind for the mind of another. Sharing was not the correct term. Surrender was more like it. Once committed, however, she had no choice. As the new mind absorbed her, her own memories reluctantly slipped from her grasp. She retained little more than her sense of self and her perspective of the situation. It was as if the two linked side by side in the manner of connected twins.

Painful as the transition was, most of what Kreindia wanted to know came within reach. With a gasp, she suddenly knew that the man and woman were Faron and Clara, apparently the mother and stepfather of this Del, her host.

The self-propelled vehicle was a fuel-burning machine, its name shortened to "car." The time period was the twenty-first century. How many years had passed since her era was something she should have easily been able to calculate, but it eluded her. Losing contact with her memories meant losing the questions that related to the solution of her plight. She feared now that these new facts were the acquisition of trivia. The claustrophobic imposition of "sharing" came with the nightmarish sense that if their combination lasted too long it would become permanent. To calm her a bit, the other girl let Kreindia keep physical control, such as it was.

Deceptively calm now, Faron said, "Don't head that way, Kreindel. Use the ramp. If you could move those scrawny arms, mark my words, you'd be in a chair that ran on your own power. But you choose to be useless. The doctor said so." Like Kreindia, Del thought of her stepfather as a jailer and her mother as a fellow slave. From Del: *Thank you, Daddy. I so appreciate my mobile prison.*

Faron's remark seemed to have awakened Clara's curiosity. "But a few minutes ago, you said—"

He glanced around to make sure no one watched, and then dealt her cheek an efficient clip that snapped her face askew.

Kreindia had already taken off on the sloping route, grateful that it led in a different direction, and disappointed when it made a complete turn back to meet her putative parents at the foot of the stairs.

Together they crossed a black expanse paved with ripe asphalt cooking in the sun. At a spot marked out in blue—a handicapped space—they halted. At that same moment she heard a buzz along with a muffled tinkle of music. Faron brought out a cell phone (Del's term for it), and said, "Yes?"

The caller spoke loudly enough for the words to leak out. "Sir, this is the receptionist from upstairs. There's a crazy man on his way down to you. I don't know what he wants, but I couldn't stop him. The doctor didn't want me to call the police, but I did anyway."

Faron said, "You did the right thing warning me." Without another word, he threw the phone back in his pocket and retrieved a set of keys and a fob that he used to elicit a chirp to unlock the white van parked in front of them.

Before they got any further, a shambling apparition approached them, dirty, bleeding and disheveled. Faron started at the sight of him almost as if he knew the man, and hastened to operate the van's lift gate.

The tall thin upstart closed quickly on the small family group in his disarrayed pullover shirt, jeans and sneakers. Crossing a loose shoelace, he stumbled and recovered without taking notice. The missed stride revealed bare ankles and a crusty re-opened wound. When Faron began to push his daughter onto the lift gate, the grimy intruder stopped the chair and swiveled her to face him.

Both of the merged young women needed only the Twenty First Century memories to realize that they had seen him once before, at Del's last visit to Dr. Nesky. And in dreams. His face could not have been gentler or sadder. With a sigh, he seemed to buckle at the knees to land in front of them.

This relative stranger said, "It's me, sweetheart, it's me. Is it you?" Tears welled over the rims of his eyes. Distraught beyond reason, this fellow was oblivious to the scene he had caused.

Faron snarled, "What the hell are you doing to my daughter?" The remark and its daggered tone could not divert the poor man.

He pleaded, "Sweetheart, can you move? Please speak to me, please move for me." He came out with it in a voice so choked with emotion that it tugged at their collective heart even though they didn't know what he hoped to gain by accosting them.

As Kreindia/ Del struggled to make sense of the mysterious figure before them, the girl's will retreated, causing everything to blur. The Second pulled back enough to give Kreindia's psyche a chance to emerge for a turn at dominance along with access to her memories. Once again she fought to hold onto both sets of information to no avail.

Herself again, Kreindia felt as though a curtain had been torn aside. Wade of Aquitaine had stood there the whole time. She knew all would be well, and they could be together if she could only muster the proper reaction.

She committed the fingers of her right hand to the joystick, thinking she might waggle the chair back and forth, or forward and back. With little more than a touch, the effort required to quirk the chair an inch, her last strength failed her. Her collapse was mental as well as physical. She'd suffered the exhaustion of trying to merge the two minds. Darkness encroached on the fringes of her vision.

Faron shouted at Wade, "She can't move, or even speak, you idiot. She's a total cripple quad nothing. What do you want from her?"

Tenderly, Wade took her limp left hand in his own and kissed her palm, his eyelashes brushing the insides of her fingers.

"I'm calling the police," said Faron.

After her brief respite, Kreindia tried moving her right hand again towards the controls, and then hesitated and changed course. For the first time since illness struck this body, she raised her trembling hand and her arm with it. It left the armrest with only a slight hesitation to ascend way in the air. Her stepfather dropped his jaw in astonishment. She fully extended her arm, and touched all five fingertips to Wade's cheek. Now she was able to cry too. As Faron's protests grew louder, she tilted her head and looked deep into his brown eyes. A teardrop ran the length of her nose.

"Oh, Wade, we made it," she said.

At once she saw the truth of her life. All gathered had come together in this manner for a reason. Somehow she had been fractured into two women. That's what the joining had to mean. Fractured, and the pieces brought side by side to bond again just as she and Wade were reunited. The alternative was that she had been born a creation of fragments, an idea she found even harder to accept. The conundrum of why she remained two people in one body had to wait.

Kreindia murmured, "We made it, we made it, we made it," until the atrophied muscles in her arms could hold no longer. Her right arm slipped first, with her hand making a clutching spasm, briefly getting hold of

Wade's shirt. Her left arm dropped like a bird dying in flight. Now she cried tears of frustration, wondering if the cage would return, limiting her to moving this chariot with her tiny magic wand, and luring the unwary to take her place in the manner of a heartless Siren.

Then she colored in shame for worrying about her condition, followed by a rush of thankfulness for being alive and with Wade. "We made it," she repeated, this time in clarity and confirmation.

Wade pulled back and brushed the dark hair away from her eyes. He laughed, "Can you say anything else?"

"I love you, Aquitainian," she whispered, using his Ninth Century name to demonstrate her identity through special knowledge of his. The declaration made her cry even more in great heaving breaths. Her tears flowed not as drops, but in a continual torrent of relief, coating her flushed skin.

A shadow came over them. Faron put his rough hand on Wade's shoulder, and squeezed as though his sharp fingers were digging for bone. Kreindia could not imagine a captive or servant anywhere in the empire subjected to more suffering than the girl and her mother endured at the hands of her unlikely father. Now Wade had been dragged into it.

"Young man, I warned you to stay away from her when you showed up at the doctor's office last time," he said. "Soon you'll see the price."

ABOUT THE AUTHOR

Ben Parris is the author of WADE OF AQUITAINE, one of the very first Kindle Best Sellers upon its debut, rising to top honors (rankings of 1, 2, and 3) in four categories for a total of more than 20 weeks in its first year and returning to that list for an encore of another six weeks in the second year. A former Scholastic columnist, published in several short story anthologies, Parris completed this first novel at the age of 36.

Ben Parris can be reached through
ben@blueberrylanebooks.com